FINE FURNITURE REPRODUCTIONS

18th Century Revivals of the 1930s & 1940s

FROM BAKER FURNITURE

77 Lower Valley Road, Atglen, PA 19310

ok is by Schiffer Pub-
lishing, Ltd. derived from the catalog published
c. 1940 by Baker Furniture, Inc. of Holland,
Michigan. Baker Furniture Inc. has not assisted
in the publication of this book, nor has Baker
Furniture Inc. authorized its publication.

ISBN: 0-7643-0125-X
Printed in China

Library of Congress Cataloging-in-Publication Data

Fine furniture reproductions : 18th century revivals of the
    1930s & 1940s from Baker Furniture.
        p. cm.
    Includes index.
    ISBN: 0-7643-0125-X
    1. Baker Furniture Company--Catalogs. 2. Furniture--
Reproduction--Catalogs. 3. Furniture--Styles--Catalogs.
    I. Schiffer Publishing Ltd.
NK2439.B38F56   1996
749.2--dc20   96-26616
                                                      CIP

Published by Schiffer Publishing Ltd.
77 Lower Valley Road
Atglen, PA 19310
Phone: (610) 593-1777
FAx: (610) 593-2002
Please write for a free catalog.
This book may be purchased from the publisher.
Please include $2.95 for shipping.
Try your bookstore first.

We are interested in hearing from authors
with book ideas on related subjects.

Contents

Introduction

When the young man from the Netherlands arrived in the United States, around 1870, he had little more than a woodworker's skills and a driving ambition. It was enough. Settling among his fellow Dutch immigrants in western Michigan, Siebe Baker began to establish himself in his adopted country, seeking out the American dream. Within a decade he was a partner in a successful business. Ten years later, in 1890, he and Henry Cook founded Cook & Baker, a wood milling operation that would become Baker Furniture, one of the most highly respected manufacturers of fine furniture.

In the earliest years they provided the materials needed by the building industry. Western Michigan and the whole midwest was experiencing rapid growth and the new residents required homes, which required doors, windows, and sashes. Strategically located for transportation and timber, and abundantly blessed with European craftsmen, the area around Grand Rapids became a center of the woodworking manufacture.

By 1893 Cook & Baker had produced its first commercially available piece of furniture, an oak desk/bookcase combination. According to Sam Burchell's *A History of Furniture: Celebrating Baker Furniture, 100 Years of Fine Reproductions*, (New York: Harry N. Abrams, Inc., Publishers, 1991) the product line in the early years followed the late 19th century fashion of golden oak, producing pieces that reflected the light, flowing lines of Art Noveau design. Bookcases, desks, buffets, china cabinets and other household pieces were introduced, and the company grew to be the largest employer in Allegan, Michigan. It had thirty employees. *(Burchell, pp. 129-130)*

In 1903 Cook & Baker became Baker & Company, in 1913 it was incorporated, and in 1915 Siebe Baker became its sole owner. It was to continue in the family for three generations.

After Siebe Bakers death in 1925, his son, Hollis S. Baker, became president of the company. As Burchell notes, under his leadership the company saw an important period of expansion and direction.

He came into the presidency with a strong sense of furniture design and of the direction he wanted the company to pursue. He was influenced, in part, by the Arts & Crafts movement in England and the United States, which had reawakened interest in the quality of the handcrafted furniture of the pre-industrial age. In the studios and workshops of Stickley, Roycroft, and others, a strong, new sense of design was developing. It emphasized a sparse beauty, utilitarian function, and, above all, quality workmanship. The challenge of Baker's vision for the future was to find a way in which the quality of handcrafting could be wedded to the practicalities of mass-manufacturing.

The other influence upon Baker was the revival of interest in period furniture. Burchell traces this revival to the Centennial Exposition of 1876 in Philadelphia. *(Burchell, pp. 6 ff.)* The celebration of the birth of a nation awakened an appreciation of the skill of the American artisans. An interest in antiques grew as did the manufacturer of reproduction and imitative furniture. Vincent Lockwood first published his classic work, *Colonial Furniture in America*, in 1901, to be revised in 1913 and 1926. Wallace Nutting published *Furniture of the Pilgrim Century* in 1924, and the classic *Furniture Treasury* in 1928. Nutting, of course, produced his own line of reproduction period furniture.

Because of this growing popularity, Baker Furniture produced three lines of American reproduction furniture in the 1920s: a line of colonial furniture introduced in 1922; a Duncan Phyfe suite in 1923; and a line of Pilgrim dining room furniture in 1926.

It was not until Hollis S. Baker brought these two movements together - high quality and historic design - that Baker Furniture Factories (as it was named in 1927) began to specialize in fine reproduction furniture. Baker traveled around

Europe seeking examples of fine furniture. He bought many pieces and had them sent back to Michigan to be used as references. For other pieces he commissioned complete measured drawings, complete down to the detail of the color of an inlay. *(Burchell, p. 132)* In addition he collected photographs, shop drawings, plaster casts, books, and old tools, anything that would be of use in producing a quality, faithful reproduction.

In 1929 Baker developed the marketing concept of the Milling Road Shops. The brainchild of William Millington, head designer at Baker, it involved the creation of a special sales area within a retail store to promote a special line of Baker reproductions. The sales area had a faux store front and featured "approximately sixty Georgian pieces that had been illustrated in *Connoisseur* magazine from 1900 to 1928." Each piece had a tag that detailed its provenance and the date of its appearance in the magazine.

This practice of identifying the historical background and provenance of a piece is carried into the catalog republished here. Though there is no publication date, in his Foreword Hollis S. Baker identifies it as "the fortieth catalog by our company" published for the fiftieth anniversary year. In it each item is illustrated with a black and white photograph. It is identified by a product number, a descriptive name, information on the history and provenance, and dimensions. For example, a tub chair on page 40 is described as:

No. 7094 Wing Chair
Adapted from an upholstered tub chair
illustrated in MacQuoid's "The History of
English Furniture." Circa 1780.
Height 40. Depth 31. Width 29.

A desk from the Milling Road Shop collection on page 145 is similarly detailed:

No. M653 Desk
Reproduced from small secretary desk illustrated
in Edgar G. Miller, Jr.'s "American
Antique Furniture" and in the collection of
Mr. Francis T. Redwood. Circa 1790-1810.
Boxwood inlays. Leather lined writing bed
folds forward to open. Size opened 28 x 36.
Base 19 x 36. Height 44.

Not only did this catalog fill its primary purpose of selling furniture, it educated the salespeople who used it. Armed with this information they were much better able to present Baker furniture to consumers who came into their shops.

In a 1923 article for *The Furniture Blue-Book* (quoted in *Burchell, p. 11-12*) Hollis S. Baker cites the wisdom of William Morris, the leader of the English Arts and Crafts movement. "Have only what you know to be useful and believe to be beautiful." Reflecting on this Baker continues:

"There is no better rule for the maker or buyer of furniture....One of the joys of manufacturing is the creative aspect of the business. It is not so hard to make beautiful things where unlimited time and money can be spent. But to bring beauty within the reach of the average man is an even higher accomplishment. It is here that an opportunity lies in the furniture trade. As usual where a serious effort is made to fulfill a demand, those who accomplish this end are able to reap a financial profit - and on this ground it is possible to bring together our commercial instincts and higher ideals."

Writing seventeen years later in the Foreword to this catalog Baker wrote:

"It is natural that there should be confusion as to what makes a truly fine reproduction, because the market is replete with poor copies of antique furniture. In order to clarify this point, we have made this...more than just a picture book. It our hope that it will be used as an authoritative guide for fine furniture as well as a sales aid. The search for unusual antiques and the painstaking care in their reproduction is not only a business with us - it is a hobby, too. The furniture shown in the pages of this book is the result of many years spent in the pursuit of this hobby. More than that it is the achievement of a half century of manufacturing furniture."

A Distinguished Collection

of

ENGLISH and FRENCH FURNITURE

of the

18th CENTURY

Compiled and Manufactured

BY

Baker Furniture, Inc.

CABINET MAKERS

10 MILLING ROAD, HOLLAND, MICHIGAN

BEING *both a Catalog and Reference Book of those designs Most Esteemed by Connoisseurs, including selections from* the 19th CENTURY

Foreword

IT IS natural that there should be confusion as to what makes a truly fine reproduction, because the market is replete with poor copies of antique furniture. In order to clarify this point, we have made this, the fortieth catalog published by our company, more than just a picture book. It is our hope that it will be used as an authoritative guide for fine furniture as well as a sales aid.

The search for unusual antiques and the painstaking care in their reproduction is not only a business with us — it is a hobby, too. The furniture shown in the pages of this book is the result of many years spent in the pursuit of this hobby. More than that, it is the achievement of a half century of manufacturing furniture, for this year marks our fiftieth anniversary. We will be pleased, if you consider this book a worthwhile memento of the occasion.

Special thanks and credit are due to those many friends, collectors, antique dealers and museums — only a few of whom can be mentioned by name — who have made it possible to assemble this material.

Hollis S. Baker

President, Baker Furniture, Inc.

A Group of Pieces from our Manor House Division

Why Do Connoisseurs Choose Baker Furniture?

Because, this furniture not only has sound intrinsic value, but it also has those *intangible values* which are essential to fine things. Connoisseurs recognize that Baker furniture is designed with a different viewpoint. It is made and finished in a totally different manner than ordinary furniture. Many of the best known editors, collectors, and other manufacturers of furniture choose Baker Furniture for their own homes. In the following pages we shall try to explain the method and policies which, we hope, justify this confidence.

"This Is Baker Furniture"

In this phrase is the assurance that here is traditional furniture, reproduced with utmost fidelity to the original, by a group of the best craftsmen in the fine furniture field. It signifies the highest standards of quality.

What Is "Quality"?

The indiscriminate use of such adjectives as "fine" and "choice," and of the word "quality" has created much confusion as to those characteristics essential to furniture worthy of such expressions. Actually it is rather difficult to explain to the layman those features which set the truly fine reproduction, with all its spirit of the original, apart from the ordinary copy. By itself, the word "quality" means little or nothing, because all quality is relative. The manufacturer of cheap furniture may call his a "quality" product and be truthful in fact if not in inference. In all furniture of *fine* quality, however, there are four essential points of equal importance—good design, good finish, sturdy construction —and an intangible quality of which we will say more later.

The Four Essentials

DESIGN — Without good design, whether elaborate or simple, furniture becomes just another functional product of no artistic worth. Good design is essential. Yet it is upon the *execution* of the design, as well as for the design itself, that true reproductions must depend for their kinship to other works of art. Major importance must be placed on whether the design has been copied from a fine model, but even more so that it be a *worthy* copy.

FINISH — How often a poor finish ruins an otherwise good piece of furniture! Although choice woods are beautiful in themselves, a good finish is essential to preserve and develop this natural beauty. No furniture can be truly fine if the finish is applied without thought to the character of the wood; or so that it impairs the fineness of figure and texture. And, no reproduction is good unless its finish is suitable to the period and preserves the mellow, glowing patine of the original — *described in more detail on page 7.*

A Dignified Georgian Mahogany Secretary-Breakfront, Ornamented with English Yew Tree Wood Inlays and Crossbandings.

CONSTRUCTION — Obviously, sound construction necessitates the use of choice materials. Durability and beauty depend on the proper selection of wood for various purposes. The mahoganies from Cuba, Central America and Peru are best and are used in Baker furniture. Their color and texture are carefully chosen. Selected hard woods are used for the solid framing of interior construction. Drawer interiors are made from quartered oak, thoroughly hand sanded on all sides. All lumber must be carefully seasoned and kiln dried to avoid warping, checking and similar ills. In good furniture, glass doors are made of individual panes, each puttied into its own small frame, instead of a single pane of glass, surmounted by a jig-sawed fret, common to inferior furniture. Each of the many hundreds of joints must be tightly "joined" and firmly glued. Such things — and countless others — are basic requirements.

Why Is Baker Furniture "Different"?

Intangibles

Baker furniture is different because it goes beyond ordinary fundamentals. It has *intangible* and *permanent* value. The dictionary describes "intangible" as something "not easily expressed . . . as, the beauty of a poem is intangible."

While these intangible qualities are readily apparent to the expert, they are sometimes not immediately seen by the less experienced eye. Differences in finish are subtle. There are many subtleties of fine craftsmanship. There is the thing called "patine" which, in antiques, comes partly with usage and the effect of light and age on the wood, and partly from countless polishings. In Baker furniture every effort is made to duplicate this effect, which contributes so much to the intangible beauty inherent in fine antiques.

Principles of Design

The consistent policy in making Baker furniture is to adhere to the highest standards of good taste. No compromise with this policy is permitted and no designs are concocted to serve a temporary commercial demand. The Baker design department is in charge of Mr. William Millington, who was trained in England, and who is an expert in traditional furniture. Continuous research is carried on to find antiques which are suitable for reproduction, and for other original source material. Chairs with intricate curves and carvings are always reproduced directly from the old pieces. Samples of leather work of the 18th Century English and French bookbinders, models of antique hardware, and plaster casts of fine carvings are used both as a guide for design and as models for the craftsman to follow. Accurate scale drawings of collectors' pieces come regularly from a Professor at the Royal College of Art in London, who is on a retainer to the Baker Company. Much of this material is now assembled in the new Baker Furniture Research Museum in Grand Rapids. It is carefully and continuously studied so that all proportions, scale of mouldings and other ornaments, and all details of design and execution will be correct. *Such care assures design of permanent worth.*

Materials and Craftsmanship

All materials in Baker furniture are carefully selected for their individual characteristics. In the making of a delicately carved Chippendale chairback, the densest Cuban mahogany procurable is used. This can readily be observed by feeling the weight of the chair. Similarly hard textured Cuban wood is used for the finely scaled door frames and wherever structural strength is essential. All face woods are selected for texture, color and for the type of figure most suited to the design. One piece of face veneer can easily cost ten times as much as another depending on the quality. Similar standards are followed in the quality of down and hair used in upholstered furniture and in finishing materials, where a button shellac is used. This shellac comes from India and is far superior to the mixed shellac generally used in commercial practice. Similar standards of quality are carried through to the smallest detail, for it is the *sum total of everything that makes a really good job.*

Old World Finish

Finish is one chief reason why Baker furniture differs from its imitators. The principle of this finish is based on the materials and methods used many years ago in England. Only specially trained men can apply it. Many of them, in the Baker shops, received their training abroad.

OLD WORLD FINISH identifies only *Baker* furniture. The name is registered at the U. S. Patent Office and is the sole property of Baker Furniture, Inc. It is applied, by skilled French polishers, with a small pad — not by spray gun or brush. The softly blended tones of color and shadings, the effects of age and the "patine" are gradually built up in a manner comparable to that in which the artist develops blank canvas into a beautiful picture. Old World Finish creates the lived-with quality of a fine antique.

Special Custom Finishes

All Baker finishes are "custom" in the sense that they are applied upon the receipt of order and are adapted to the requirements of a particular piece. No finished stock is kept on hand. Specifically, however, by "custom" we mean those finishes in which the toning, coloring and "antiquing" are carried on to a greater degree than in the case of standard Old World Finishes. The many added polishings, the greater variety of tone values and the additional ageing, give to these "custom" finishes the effects of fine old pieces — which can be varied in color or amount of antiquing to suit the preference of your customers.

Fine Leather Tops
Tooled in the Traditional Manner

There is something about fine old leather, richly polished and expertly tooled, that is as pleasing, yet as hard to describe, as the gleam of choice silver. It is to recreate this "something" that Baker has worked for many years. Today, the leather tops on Baker furniture compare favorably with the best work of the 18th Century craftsmen. All of them are made from the finest top-grain steerhide; individually toned and polished; and, finally, tooled in the traditional manner with genuine gold leaf. The tooling designs are reproductions from original work of the old English and French bookbinders.

Crown Glass

This detail shows the interesting effect of reflections in crown glass.

Baker Furniture, Inc., are the only furniture manufacturers in America licensed to use crown glass. This unique product is used in all pieces in the Manor House division, where glass is required, and is available at a moderate additional cost on any cabinet in the regular Baker lines.

THE ENCYCLOPEDIA AMERICANA SAYS: "Crown glass is used . . . for optical instruments, in order to destroy the disagreeable effect of the aberration of colors . . . This glass is much used for windows, especially for art work, where its peculiarly brilliant surface makes it most acceptable."

A disk of crown glass, held by the blower at the end of his "punty" — ready for cutting into individual panes, for cabinet work. (Photograph taken in England.)

A Rare and Exclusive Product

Crown glass is made only in England and by just one firm. It has a slightly convex surface with slight irregularities, such as faint whorls and minute air bubbles (similar to those in fine Waterford glass) which give it the picturesque character of old glass. Because of this "texture" it reflects light in a peculiarly brilliant manner and has a distinctive crystalline clarity.

Making Crown Glass

The methods and formula used in making crown glass date back more than 200 years, to the time when it was one of England's major industries. Crown glass is hand blown. When the molten globule is removed from the furnace at the end of the "punty" or blow pipe it is kept whirling until it flattens out into a disk, as shown in the illustration above. As the glass does not undergo any mechanical flattening process, none of its original fire polish is lost.

A Group of Baker Reproductions of 18th Century English Pieces.

Living Room Furniture In the ENGLISH Tradition

In this Renascent period of American interior design and decoration, when all furniture styles have been greatly improved, it is sometimes difficult to separate those things which have only the semblance of correctness from those which are truly fine and genuine. In behalf of the authenticity of the furniture shown in this section, and throughout the book, it should be noted that a large number of these models have been reproduced directly from antiques purchased in England and France by Mr. Hollis S. Baker; and the balance from carefully studied drawings of pieces in museums or reference books.

Among the models shown are several of Regency style, to which we would like to draw your particular attention. Many crimes have been committed in the name of Regency, for, of all styles, it is one of the most intangible and difficult for the amateur. It is seldom that complete Regency rooms have been successfully done and the value of Regency pieces lies mainly in their use as "accents." Used for this purpose, they do much to leaven a Georgian room which might otherwise be too stereotyped. A similar purpose is served by the use of occasional pieces with painted decorations.

Especial note should be taken of the upholstered furniture shown in this catalog. These pieces are carefully scaled to harmonize with the wood furniture. They are finely tailored and filled with choicest goose down and curled horse hair.

Georgian Mahogany Group

No. 1902 Coffee Table
The details of the base of this coffee table were adapted from an English Regency X bench imported from England and now in the Baker collection. Leather top.

Top 25 x 25. Height 20.

NOTE: No. 1902½ same table with decorated wood top.

No. 1904 Lamp Table
Adapted from a late 18th Century table in the Robert Stanford collection, Brighton, England. Leather top.

Top 20 x 20. Height 26.

NOTE: No. 1904½ same table with wood top.

No. 1899 Breakfront Cabinet
Adapted from a pine "Kent" bookcase illustrated in British Art Magazine, "Old Furniture."

Width 68. Depth 13. Height 86.

No. 1944 Hanging Shelf
Adapted from a hanging cabinet in Cescinsky's book "From Gothic to Sheraton." Circa 1780. Yew tree inlay.

Width 15. Depth 7. Height 36.

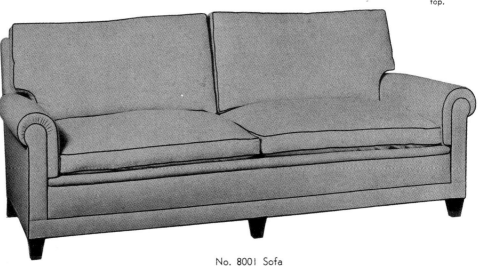

No. 8001 Sofa
A comfortable sofa of English style. A similar piece is owned by the Duke and Duchess of Windsor.

Length 84. Depth 37. Height 34.

Georgian Mahogany Group

No. 9009 Wing Chair
Reproduced from an 18th Century wing chair, a similar one of which is in Essex Institute, Salem, Mass.
Width 32. Depth 32. Height 46.

No. 1939 Sofa Table
Reproduced from an early 19th Century mahogany Sofa table with brass inlay from a private collection in Baltimore, Maryland. Brass inlays.
Top closed 25 x 40. Top open 25 x 64. Height 29.
NOTE: No. 1939½ same table of rosewood.

No. 1954 Coffee Tables
Reproduced from a Chinese table in the collection of a Chicago antique dealer. Similar pieces are illustrated in "Chinese Furniture" published in London by Benn Brothers, Ltd. Mahogany or black and gold.
Top 20 x 20. Height 17.
NOTE: No. 1954½ same table with mirror top.
(Antiqued mirror available if desired.)
NOTE: No. 1955 same table 13" high — see page 52.

No. 1780 Commode
Regency. An adaptation of an early 19th Century cupboard, the original of which was made of Rosewood, illustrated in "Regency Furniture" by Mr. Jourdain. Circa 1820.
Top 9½ x 46. Height 33.

No. 1913 Nest of Tables
The details of these tables were adapted from a late 18th Century stand in the Robert Stanford collection, Brighton, England. Leather top on each table.
Top 18 x 24. Height 25.
NOTE: No. 1913½ same Nest of Tables with wood tops and yew tree inlays.

Georgian Mahogany Group

No. 9024 Wing Chair
Adapted from a wing chair in the possession of Mr. I. Sack, Boston, Mass. Circa 1750.

Width 34. Depth 29. Height 38.

No. 355 Wall Mirror
Chippendale. Reproduced from one purchased from Hardringham Antique Shop, Brompton Road, London, England, and now in the Baker collection.
Finished Antique Pine, Antique Gold or Gold Leaf.

Plate 17 x 28. Height 43.

No. 1905 Dumbwaiter
Reproduced from an 18th Century dumbwaiter at "Denston Hall," Suffolk, England. Circa 1760.
Top Shelf 16 x 16.
Bottom shelf 24 x 24. Middle shelf 20 x 20.
Height 41.
NOTE: No. 1905½ same piece — two tier. Height 30.

No. 1929 Breakfront Bookcase
Reproduced from an original antique model found in New England and now a part of the Baker collection. Made in pine or mahogany.

Width 98. Depth 18. Height 85.

No. 1908 Hobby Table
Reproduced from a decorated hobby cabinet in the possession of the Maryland Historical Society, Baltimore.
Top 19 x 19. Height 27.
NOTE: No. 1908½ same table decorated — photograph on request.

No. 9004 Sofa
A typical English Tuxedo sofa.
Length 77. Depth 33. Height 30.

No. 1909 Lamp Table
Reproduced from a decorated hobby cabinet in the possession of the Maryland Historical Society, Baltimore. Leather top.
Top 19 x 19. Height 27.
NOTE: No. 1909½ same table with wood top.

No. 1918 Cocktail Table
The details of this table were reproduced from an early 19th Century dining table. Circa 1810. Leather top.
Top 22 x 40. Height 17½.

No. 757 Chair
Adapted from a Georgian settee in the possession of the Earl of Dysart at Ham House. Circa 1720.
Width 28. Depth 29. Height 39.

No. 1730 Desk
Hepplewhite. Reproduced from an original tambour top table desk in the collection of Mrs. John Gross. Leather top.
Top 25 x 54. Height 34.
NOTE: No. 1731 desk same piece.
Top 25 x 44.

Georgian Mahogany Group

No. 1774 Desk

Adapted from a desk owned by Owen Evans Thomas, at 20 Dover Street, London, England, and illustrated in the Connoisseur magazine. Leather top. Yew tree inlays.

Lower two right hand drawers single filing compartment.

NOTE: No. 1773 desk same piece without yew tree inlay.

NOTE: No. 1775 desk same size piece of pine. See page 32.

No. 2979 Arm Chair

Reproduced from a Sheraton decorated arm chair imported from England and now in a private Eastern collection. Circa 1800. Mahogany or painted and decorated.
Width 22½. Depth 22. Height 32.
NOTE: Side chair to match — see page 99.

No. 1903 Coffee Table

Adapted from a Chinese Chippendale table in the Cooper-Union Museum, New York. Leather top.
Top 23 x 30. Height 19.
NOTE: No. 1903½ same piece with decorated wood tray.

No. 9032 Wing Chair

Adapted from an English wing chair now in the Cooper-Union Museum, New York.
Width 30. Depth 30. Height 36.

No. 1742 Commode

Reproduced from a Hepplewhite half round commode illustrated in the Connoisseur magazine and belonging to Owen Evans Thomas, an antique dealer in Dover Street, London, England.
Top 17 x 36. Height 34.
NOTE. No. 1742½ same commode without marquetry inlays.

Georgian Mahogany Group

No. 1272 Chest

Reproduced from the base of an original Hepplewhite chest of drawers purchased in London, England, for the Baker collection. Circa 1775. Leather-lined pull-out slide.

Top 20 x 33. Height 31.

NOTE: No. 1181 same chest without yew tree inlay — see page 91.

No. 9037 Chair

A typical English lounge chair.
Width 33. Depth 36. Height 33.

No. 1921 Cocktail Table

The details of this table were copied from a side table imported from China and in the possession of O. Roche, Esquire, France. Leather top.

Top 22 x 40. Height 17.

NOTE: No. 1921½ same table with decorated wood top. Photograph on request.

No. 7085 Love Seat

Adapted from an original Hepplewhite sofa by permission of the owner, George Blundell, an English antique dealer.
Width 54. Depth 27. Height 35.

No. 1793 Desk

Reproduced from a Sheraton desk purchased in England and now in the Baker collection. Leather lined writing bed. Yew-wood inlay.

Base 21 x 27. Height 41.

NOTE: No. 1003 same desk without inlay on legs and drawer fronts. Photograph on request.

No. 7082 Sofa

Reproduced from an original model of the
late 18th Century imported from England
by an American collector.
Width 87. Depth 35. Height 36.

No. 1567 Lamp Table

Reproduced from a sewing table sold by the
American Art Gallery, New York. Circa 1800.
Top 18 x 18. Height 28.

No. 1915 Coffee Table

Adapted from a Sheraton table in the pos-
session of Debenham & Freebody, London,
England. Leather top.
Top 20 x 30. Height 18.

No. 9042 Chair
Width 27. Depth 29. Height 33.

No. 1889 Cabinet

Adapted from a Sheraton breakfront book-
case illustrated in "English Furniture of the
Georgian Period."
Width 67. Depth 13. Height 86.

Georgian Mahogany Group

No. 1733 Desk

Adapted from a Chippendale desk imported from England and sold by the American Art Association: Leather top. Yew-wood inlay.

Top 28 x 48. Height 30.

NOTE: Lower two right hand drawers single filing compartment.

No. 1762 Drop Leaf Table

Reproduced from an early 19th Century drop leaf table of the Sheraton School purchased in England and now in the Baker collection. Leather top.

Top closed 20 x 24. Top open 20 x 42. Height 28.

No. 9016 Chair

Width 27. Depth 30. Height 33.

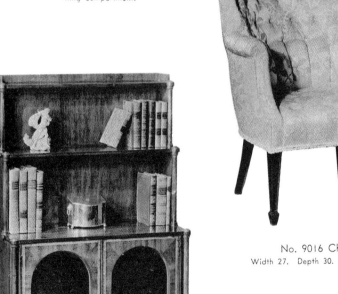

No. 1740 Bookcase

Adapted from an English Regency open bookcase at Denston Hall, England. Circa 1810. Yew-wood inlays.

Top 12 x 27. Height 44½.

No. 1588 Chest

Reproduced from a small Sheraton chest brought from England for the Baker collection. Yew-wood.

Top 16 x 27. Height 28.

NOTE: 1588½ Chest same piece in Mahogany with Yew-wood inlays.

Georgian Mahogany Group

No. 1566 Writing Table

Adapted from a writing table in an English collection and illustrated in the magazine, "Connoisseur." Leather top.

Top 24 x 42. Height 35.

No. 9011 Chair

Adapted from a typical English lounge chair.

Width 27.   Depth 36.   Height 35.

NOTE: No. 9030 same chair with tight back.

No. 1753 Pembroke Table

Reproduced from a Hepplewhite table purchased in England, and of which there are many similar models in his book, "The Cabinet Maker and Upholsterer's Guide," published in 1794. Yew-wood inlays.

Top closed 17 x 26.   Height 29.
Top open 35 x 26.

No. 1760 Chest

Adapted from an antique bachelor's chest in the collection of Mrs. Frank Leonard and formerly owned by the Ackerman Galleries. Yew-wood inlay.

Top 13 x 29.   Height 30.

NOTE: No. 960 same piece without yew tree inlays — see page 47.

No. 8004 Wing Chair

An unusual Chippendale wing chair copied from the details found among the records of an old English cabinetmaker.

Width 32.   Depth 32.   Height 42.

No. 1714 Drum Table

Reproduced from an inlaid Sheraton drum table. Circa 1790, found in Richmond, Virginia, but probably made in England. Yew-wood inlay. Leather top.

Top 32 x 32.   Height 29.

NOTE: No. 914 same table without yew tree inlay — see page 45.

No. 1517 Butler's Tray

Reproduced from an antique tray-on-stand of the late 18th Century, the original of which is now in the Baker collection.

Top 17 x 36.   Height 27.

No. 1756 Nest of Tables

Copied from a set of tables in the possession of Mrs. Stileman, London, England. The largest table has a Yew-wood top crossbanded with Mahogany.

Top 12 x 22.   Height 25.

No. 1763 Breakfront Secretary Bookcase

Adapted from the center section of a large mahogany bookcase in five compartments from the board room of "English Country Life." Yew-wood inlays.

Base 16 x 60.   Height 81.

Top drawer secretary desk with leather lined writing bed.

No. 9039 Lounge Chair

Width 29.   Depth 36.   Height 31.

No. 1713 Sofa Table

Copied from an English sofa table of the early 19th Century which is in the collection of an antique dealer in Albemarle Street, London, England. Yew-wood inlays.

Top closed 27 x 37.   Open 27 x 58.
Height 28.

NOTE: No. 913 same table without yew tree inlay — see page 41.

No. 1592½ Commode

Sheraton. Reproduced from a small commode-bookcase brought from England for the Baker collection. Yew tree inlays

Top 13 x 21.   Height 30.

NOTE: No. 1592 same commode in yew tree — photograph on request.

No. 1570 Butler's Tray

Adapted from an original English tray-on-stand brought to this country for the Baker collection.

Top 20 x 27.   Height 22.

No. 1503 Chair

Adapted from an early 19th Century elbow chair purchased in England and now in the Baker collection.

Black and Gold or Mahogany.

Width 24. Depth 23. Height 36.

No. 1539 Server

Reproduced from a card table of Sheraton influence now in the Baker collection. A similar one is illustrated by Charles Over Cornelius in "Furniture Masterpieces." Yew-wood inlay.

Top closed 17 x 36.   Open 34 x 36.
Height 30.

Georgian Mahogany Group

No. 7083 Sofa
Reproduced from a late Sheraton sofa, the
original of which is now in the possession
of an eastern importer. Circa 1810.
Width 74.   Depth 29.   Height 34.

No. 1488 Wine Cooler
Reproduced by permission from an English
wine cooler in the collection of Mrs. Van
Leer Wills. Circa 1749.
Top 12 x 12.   Height 25.
NOTE: Removable Copper Lining.

No. 1250 Cocktail Table
Adapted from a mahogany drinking table,
the property of Miss Tyndall, and illustrated
in MacQuoid's "A History of English Furniture." Circa 1790.
Top 21 x 48.   Open 35 x 48.
Height 16.

No. 1984 Wall Bracket
Adapted from an original carved bracket in
our collection typical of the highly devel-
oped work of the 18th Century carvers.
Antique Gold.
Height 14   Width 9.
NOTE: Bracket available, either right or left.

No. 1899 Arm Chair
Reproduced from a Hepplewhite arm chair
in a private Eastern collection. Walnut or
mahogany.
Width 25.   Depth 25.   Height 37.
NOTE: Side chair to match — see page 63.

No. 1726 Bookcase
Reproduced from a Mahogany cabinet, one
of a pair, from a private collection shown
at Messrs. Christie's, London, England. Circa
1790.
Base 18 x 27.   Height 83.

Georgian Mahogany Group

No. 720 Chair
Adapted from a late Sheraton model of the 19th Century.
Width 23. Depth 23. Height 35.

No. 1729 Breakfront Secretary Bookcase
Copied from an English Breakfront Cabinet of the late 18th Century, now in a private collection near Bethlehem, Pennsylvania. Leather lined writing bed. Yew-wood inlays.
Base 15½ x 76. Height 94.

No. 193 Coffee Table
Adapted from a Sheraton table in the possession of Debenham & Freebody, London, England. Leather top.
Top 20 x 30. Height 18.
NOTE: Also available without metal gallery.

No. 1565 Butler's Tray
Reproduced from an original tray-on-stand brought from England for the Baker collection.
Top 22 x 30. Height 30.
NOTE: No. 1570 same piece coffee table height — see page 20.

No. 1761 Drum Table
The original of this drum table is in the Hope collection, London, England. Circa 1810. Yew-wood inlay. Leather top.
Top 38 x 38. Height 28.

Georgian Mahogany Group

No. 1016 Cocktail Table
Adapted from a Chippendale card table illustrated in MacQuoid's History of English Furniture.
Top 26 x 42. Height 15.
Leather Top.

No. 730 Chair
Copy of an original English chair now in the Cooper-Union Museum, New York
Width 33. Height 44. Depth 34.

No. 360 Wall Mirror
A Georgian mirror reproduced from one purchased from Hardringham Antique Shop, Brompton Road, London, England, and now in the Baker collection.
Finished Antique Pine, Antique Gold or Gold Leaf.
Plate 28 x 32. Height 42.

No. 1006 Corner Cupboard
Copy of Hepplewhite cabinet purchased in England and now in our collection. Similar one in the Victoria and Albert Museum, South Kensington, England.
Width 26. Height 78.

No. 1033½ Desk
Adapted from a Georgian desk imported from England, and sold by the American Art Association. Leather top.
Top 29 x 49. Height 30.
NOTE: Lower right-hand drawers single filing compartment.
NOTE: No. 1785 desk same piece top 26 x 46 — photograph on request.

Georgian Mahogany Group

No. 1751 Sofa Table

Sheraton. Adapted from an original sofa table owned by Gill and Reigate, London, England. Yew-wood inlays.

Top closed 24 x 36. Top open 24 x 57. Height 28.

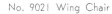

No. 1754 Tea Table

An English tea table with serpentine top and fretted corner brackets in the manner of Hepplewhite. Circa 1785. Leather Top.

Top 20 x 30. Height 25.

No. 9021 Wing Chair

Adapted from an original wing chair in our collection. This type of chair was used both in England and America during the 18th Century.

Width 28. Depth 28. Height 38.

No. 1746 Pembroke Table

This table is reproduced from a Sheraton Pembroke table in the collection of Mr. A. Hanney of England. Circa 1785. Yew-wood inlay.

Top closed 19 x 30. Open 30 x 37. Height 28.

No. 1712 Desk

Pedestal desk of the Chippendale school reproduced from a collection at "Bury-Knowle", Headington, Oxon, England. Yew-wood inlays. Leather top.

Note: Lower two right hand drawers single filing compartment.

Top 32 x 60. Height 30.

NOTE: No. 912 desk same piece without yew tree inlay.

Georgian Mahogany Group

No. 1981 Chest
Reproduced from a Chippendale small chest in the collection of a New York Importer. Top 20 x 35½. Height 32.
NOTE: No. 1972 same chest with yew tree inlays. Photograph on request.

No. 1759 Drop Leaf Table
Adapted from an English sofa table in the Bethnal Green Museum, London, England. Yew-wood inlays.
Top closed 16 x 26. Top open 16 x 40. Height 24.
NOTE: No. 1456 same piece in yew tree. Photograph on request.

No. 7006 Chair
Adapted from a late Sheraton chair illustrated in Herbert E. Binstead's "English Chairs." Circa 1800. Paint or Mahogany. Width 25. Depth 26. Height 35.

No. 1708 Nest of Tables
Adapted from a set of tables in the possession of Mrs. Stileman, London, England. The top of the large table is of Yew-wood, cross-banded with Mahogany.
Top 15 x 26. Height 25.
NOTE: No. 1108 same nest of tables with leather top on largest table. See page 47.

No. 1549 Cabinet
Adapted from a late Georgian wing front cabinet in an English collection. Circa 1795. Yew-wood inlays. Leather lined writing bed.
Base 18 x 52. Height 81.
NOTE: No. 1099 cabinet same piece without yew tree inlays. See page 73.

Georgian Mahogany Group

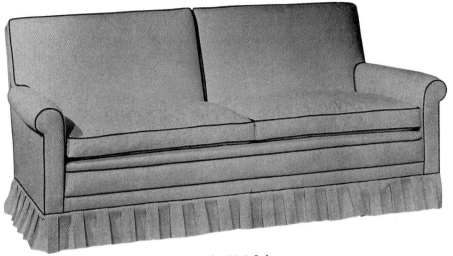

No. 9048 Sofa
A comfortable sofa of English style.
Length 76. Depth 36. Height 33.

No. 2989 Commode
Adapted from a small 18th Century Sheraton commode in the possession of Debenham and Freebody, London, England, illustrated in the Connoisseur magazine. Satinwood inlay.
Top 11 x 20. Height 27.

No. 1914 Coffee Table
The base of this table was reproduced from an X frame in the collection of the Duke of Northumberland, Syon House, England. Circa 1805.
Top 23 x 31. Height 21.
NOTE: No. 1914½ same table with custom decorated tray.

No. 1795
Breakfront Secretary Bookcase
Adapted from a Hepplewhite breakfront secretary bookcase imported from England and recently sold at a New York antique sale. Leather lined writing bed.
Width 56. Depth 15. Height 83.
NOTE: No. 1794 same piece in mahogany.
See page 43.

No. 9026 Lounge Chair
Width 28. Depth 36. Height 33.

Georgian Mahogany Group

No. 7067 Wing Chair
Reproduced from a Chippendale chair illustrated in the Connoisseur Magazine, the property of Gill & Reigate of London, England.
Width 32. Depth 32. Height 44.

No. 7072 Chair
Motifs taken from a Chippendale chair illustrated in Herbert Cescinsky's "English Furniture of the 18th Century."
Width 26. Depth 29. Height 40.

No. 1906 Dumbwaiter
Adapted from an 18th Century dumbwaiter at "Denston Hall," Suffolk, England. Circa 1760.
Lower shelf 24 x 24. Middle shelf 20 x 20. Top shelf 16 x 16. Height 41.
NOTE: No. 1906½ same table — two tier. Height 30.

No. 1912 Nest of Tables
Adapted from a Sheraton stand purchased in England and now in the Baker collection. Leather top on all three tables.
Top 17 x 22. Height 25.
NOTE: No. 1912½ same nest of tables with leather top on largest table and mahogany top on other two tables.

No. 1777 Desk
Reproduced from an 18th Century kneehole desk designed by Chippendale and illustrated in his "Cabinet Makers' and Gentlemen's Directory." Leather top. Lower two right-hand drawers single filing compartment.
Top 34 x 60. Height 30.
NOTE: No. 1997 same desk — 36 x 66.
No. 1998 same desk — 38 x 72.
Photographs on request.
NOTE: No. 1152 same desk without yew tree inlay — see page 36.

Georgian Mahogany Group

No. 6994 Wing Chair
Copy of an original English chair now in the Cooper-Union Museum, New York.
Width 29. Depth 31. Height 42.

No. 1975½ Desk
Adapted from a Georgian desk belonging to Miss Scholfield and illustrated in Mac-Quoid's "Age of Satinwood." Leather top. Walnut.
Top 24 x 48. Height 30.
NOTE: No. 1975 desk same piece in mahogany with boxwood line inlay.
No. 1985 same desk in mahogany with yew tree crossbanding. Photographs on request

No. 1715 Fern Stand
Adapted from a late 18th Century table in the possession of Debenham & Freebody, London.
Top 18 x 24. Height 25.
NOTE: No. 1715½ same table without flower well.

No. 1975½ Desk — Back View

No. 7089 Settee
Details for this chair back settee were reproduced from a Chippendale chair purchased in England and now in the Baker collection. Similar models are illustrated by Cescinsky in his book on English Furniture.
Length 50. Depth 25. Height 38.

No. 9012 Lounge Chair
Width 32. Depth 35. Height 32.
No. 9029 Chair—Same chair with tight back.

Georgian Mahogany Group

No. 1916 Lamp Table
Adapted from a Sheraton table in the possession of Debenham & Freebody, London, England. Leather top.
Top 20 x 30. Height 26.

No. 8002 Love Seat
An early 19th Century type sofa similar to one illustrated by M. Jourdain in his book on Regency furniture.
Length 63. Depth 34. Height 33.

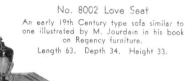

No. 1953 Cocktail Table
Reproduced from a Chinese table in the collection of a Chicago antique dealer. Similar tables are illustrated in "Chinese Furniture" published by Benn Brothers, Ltd., London, England. Antique white and gold or black and gold. Leather top.
Top 25 x 38. Height 15.
NOTE: No. 1953½ same table with mirror top.

No. 747 Chair
Reproduced from a late Sheraton Chair purchased in England. Similar model illustrated in MacQuoid's Dictionary.
Width 18. Height 33. Depth 16.

No. 9015 Lounge Chair
Width 27. Depth 37. Height 33.

No. 1945 Card Table
Adapted from a Sheraton table, illustrated in the Burlington magazine, London, England. Leather top.
Top 32 x 32. Height 28.

Georgian Mahogany Group

No. 9005 Love Seat
Length 55. Depth 34. Height 33.

No. 1439 Arm Chair
Reproduced from a French Hepplewhite
easy chair in a private collection in Queen's
Road, Dalston, England.
Width 26. Depth 29. Height 37.

No. 180 Tea Table
Adapted from a small rosewood table
illustrated by M. Jourdain in his book on
Regency furniture. In the style of 1800.
Leather top. Candle slides both ends.
Top 17 x 30. Height 24.

No. 1976 Desk — Back View

No. 9023 Chair
Width 28. Depth 32. Height 34.

No. 1976 Desk
Adapted from a late 18th Century oval
desk of the Sheraton school. Leather top.
Yew tree inlays.
Top 32 x 48. Height 30.
NOTE: Interior of each end accommodates
stationery, etc.

No. 9020 Chair

Adapted from a Chippendale chair illustrated in Herbert Cescinsky's book on English Furniture. Circa 1760.
Width 26. Depth 31. Height 36.

No. 7088 Bench

Reproduced from a Chippendale window seat recently sold at the American Art Association Galleries, New York.
Overall width 49. Depth 16.
Height of arm 26.
Length of seat 38. Height of seat 18.

No. 1509 Table

Reproduced from a Rosewood sofa table banded and inlaid with satinwood from the collection of Messrs. Harris, London antique dealers. Circa 1800. Mahogany or Rosewood, Plain or Decorated.
Top 17 x 30. Height 24.

No. 1919 Library Steps

Reproduced from an original antique model purchased from a New York importer and now in the Baker collection. Leather top on each step.
Width 17. Depth 28. Height 26.
NOTE: Storage compartment beneath hinged top and middle steps.

No. 9046 Chair

Reproduced from a late 18th Century chair in the collection of a Chicago antique dealer.
Width 26. Depth 29. Height 38.

No. 1157 Desk

A rare miniature mahogany kneehole desk of the early 18th Century from the collection of Owen Evan-Thomas, London, England. Illustrated in the Connoisseur magazine. Leather lined writing slide.
Top 20 x 35. Height 29.
NOTE: No. 1157½ same piece with yew tree crossbanding.

Georgian Mahogany Group

No. 1775 Desk

Adapted from a Georgian desk imported from England and sold by the American Art Association. Leather top. Lower two right hand drawers single filing compartment.

Top 26 x 44. Height 30.

NOTE: No. 1774 desk same piece in mahogany with yew tree inlays — see page 14. No. 1773 same desk in mahogany without inlay.

No. 9047 Wing Chair

Adapted from an English porter's chair of the 18th Century, illustrated in the Connoisseur Magazine.

Width 30. Depth 33. Height 40.

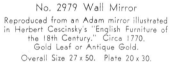

No. 2979 Wall Mirror

Reproduced from an Adam mirror illustrated in Herbert Cescinsky's "English Furniture of the 18th Century." Circa 1770. Gold Leaf or Antique Gold.

Overall Size 27 x 50. Plate 20 x 30.

No. 9041 Lounge Chair

Width 32. Depth 36. Height 30.

NOTE: No. 9038 same chair with buttoned back — photograph on request.

No. 7047 Chair

Width 28. Depth 28. Height 33.

Georgian Mahogany Group

No. 9002 Sofa

Chippendale English 18th Century. Reproduced from one sold at a New York antique
sale by the American Art Association.
Length 78.   Depth 33.   Height 35.

No. 1941 Dumb Waiter

A late 18th Century dumb waiter adapted
from one illustrated in MacQuoid's "The
Dictionary of English Furniture," from
Denston Hall, England. Circa 1790.
Upper top 16 x 16.   Lower 21 x 21.
Height 30.

No. 1920½ Cocktail Table

The details of this table were copied from a
side table imported from China and in the
possession of O. Roche, Esq., France.
NOTE: No. 1920 same table with leather top.
Photographs on request.

No. 705 Wing Chair

Adapted from chair in possession of Mr. I.
Sack, Boston. Circa 1750.
Width 34.   Depth 30.   Height 41.

No. 1490½ Commode

Regency. An adaptation of an early 19th
Century cupboard, the original of which was
illustrated in "Regency Furniture" by M.
Jourdain. Circa 1820.
Top 10 x 46.   Height 33.

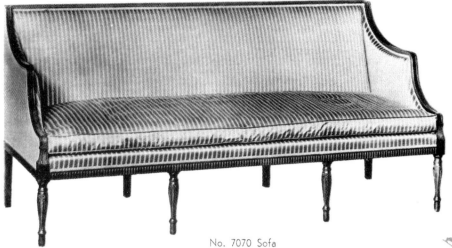

No. 7070 Sofa

Reproduced from a Hepplewhite sofa imported from England by a Chicago collector.
Length 78. Depth 33. Height 36.
NOTE: No. 7070 Sofa made both in Mahogany and Beech for natural finish.

No. 1113 Fern Stand

Adapted from a late 18th Century table
in the possession of Debenham & Freebody,
London.

Top 18 x 24. Height 26.

NOTE: No. 1113½ same table without
flower well.

No. 1129 Breakfront Secretary
Bookcase

Copied from an English bookcase of the late
18th Century now in a private collection near
Bethlehem, Pennsylvania.

Base 15 x 76. Height 85.
Leather lined writing bed.

No. 1148 Stand

Reproduction of an English imported basin
stand. Similar model is illustrated in Mac-
Quoid's "Dictionary of English Furniture."
Circa 1780.

Top 11 x 11. Height 35.

No. 907 Pie Crust Tilt Table

English 18th Century pie crust table with
revolving and tilting top. From the collection
of H. Blairman, Harrogate, England.

Top 32 x 32.   Height 29.

No. 9006 Love Seat

Reproduced from a Chippendale love seat
sold at Christy's Galleries, London, England.
Circa 1730.

Length 59.   Depth 33.   Height 34.

No. 1453 Pembroke Table

Reproduced from a Hepplewhite table purchased in England, and of which there are
many similar models in his book, "The Cabinet Maker and Upholsterer's Guide,"
published in 1794.

Top closed 17 x 26.   Height 29.
Top open 35 x 26.

NOTE: No. 1753 same table with yew tree
inlays — see page 18.

No. 990 Folding Table

Reproduced from original imported model.
Similar table is illustrated in MacQuoid's
Dictionary.

Top 25 x 36.   Height 18.

No. 743 Chair

Reproduced from Queen Anne chair purchased in England, and now in our collection.
Similar model belongs to Sir George Donald-
son, and is illustrated in MacQuoid's
Dictionary.

Width 29.   Height 43.   Depth 27.

No. 1033 Desk

Adapted from a Chippendale desk imported
from England, and sold by the American Art
Association. Leather top.

Top 28 x 48.   Height 30.

NOTE: Lower two right-hand drawers single
filing compartment.

NOTE: No. 1033½ same desk of pine — see
page 23.

Georgian Mahogany Group

No. 1152 Desk

Reproduction of an 18th Century kneehole desk designed by Chippendale and illustrated in his "Cabinet Makers' and Gentlemen's Directory." Leather top. Lower two right-hand drawers single filing compartment. Mahogany or walnut.

Top 34 x 60. Height 30.

NOTE: No. 1992 same desk — 36 x 66.
No. 1993 same desk — 38 x 72.
Photographs on request.

NOTE: No. 1777 same desk with yew tree inlay — see page 27.

No. 726 Chair

Reproduced from a Sheraton chair imported from England and now in the Baker collection. Beech.

Width 21. Depth 21. Height 31.

No. 1409 Hanging Shelf

A Chippendale wall shelf, illustrated in the Connoisseur Magazine by a London antique dealer.

Width 25. Height 37.

No. 1951½ Cocktail Table

The details of this table were reproduced from a directoire table desk in the collection of a Chicago antique dealer. Parquet top.

Top closed 20 x 36. Top open 20 x 50. Height 18.

NOTE: No. 1951 same table with leather top.
NOTE: No. 1952½ same table. 30 x 30 closed — see page 48.

No. 8012 Chair

Reproduced with exception of swivel base from the original Judge Cushing chair in the old Boston State House. It is said to be the chair in which Judge Cushing sat when presiding at the trial of the British soldiers in the Boston Massacre. Circa 1780.

Width 23. Depth 22. Height 32.

No. 721 Love Seat

Copy of an English imported piece of the Chippendale period.

Length 60. Depth 22. Height 38.

Georgian Mahogany Group

No. 754 Chair
Reproduced from a Chippendale chair illustrated in Herbert Cescinsky's book on English Furniture. Circa 1760.
Width 27. Height 35. Depth 32.

No. 1138 Cocktail Table (open)
Motifs taken from a Sheraton sofa table in the possession of Lady Assleton Smith, London, England. Leather top.
Top open 21 x 63. Height 16.
NOTE: Removable copper tray is stored underneath table when it is closed.
NOTE: No. 1138½ same piece with leather top tray.

No. 1138 Cocktail Table
Motifs taken from a Sheraton sofa table in the possession of Lady Assleton Smith, London, England. Leather top.
Top closed 21 x 40. Height 16.
NOTE: Removable copper tray is stored underneath table when it is closed.
NOTE: No. 1138½ same piece with leather top tray.

No. 1564 Piecrust Table
A Chippendale piecrust table adapted from an original in the Blairman collection at Harrogate, England.
Top 29 x 29. Height 27.

No. 7026 Sofa
Adapted from one in a London interior. Illustrated in "The Connoisseur" magazine.
Length 80. Depth 35. Height 34.
NOTE: No. 6991 same sofa with tight back. Photograph on request.

No. 1971 Desk

Adapted from a George II kneehole desk,
illustrated in Symond's "English Furniture."
Leather top. Walnut.
Top 28 x 48. Height 30.

No. 1438 Arm Chair

Copied by permission from a Georgian arm
chair in a private collection in Queen's
Road, Dalston, England.
Width 24. Depth 27. Height 37.

No. 7091 Stool
Top 30 x 30. Height 18.
NOTE: No. 7091½ Stool.
Top 36 x 36. Height 18.

No. 1910 Record Cabinet

Adapted from a late 18th Century cabinet
in a private New York collection.
Width 26. Depth 17. Height 38.
NOTE: Piece will accommodate 18 —
12" x 14" record albums.

No. 9008 Wing Chair
Width 31. Depth 31. Height 38.

Georgian Mahogany Group

No. 7058 Sofa
Length 80. Depth 36. Height 36.

.No. 1907 Book Stand
Reproduced from a drum stand. Circa 1780, in the possession of a Bond street antique dealer, London, England. Leather top.
Top 20 x 20. Height 24.
NOTE: No. 1907½ same piece decorated. Photograph on request.

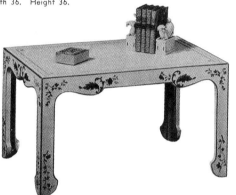

No. 1922 Cocktail Table
The details of this table were copied from a side table imported from China and in the possession of O. Roche, Esq., France. Antique white and gold decorated or black and gold decorated. Leather top.
Top 20 x 30. Height 17.
NOTE: No. 1922½ same table with wood top decorated.

No. 9043 Chair
A small, comfortable lounge chair with loose down cushion back.
Width 27. Depth 32. Height 32.

No. 742 Chair
Reproduced from a Sheraton chair purchased in England, and now in our collection. Similar model is illustrated in Lenygon's Book on English Furniture.
Width 30. Height 42. Depth 29.

Georgian Mahogany Group

No. 7094 Wing Chair
Adapted from an upholstered tub chair illustrated in MacQuoid's "The History of English Furniture." Circa 1780.
Height 40. Depth 31. Width 29.

No. 1490 Commode
Regency. An adaption of an early 19th Century cupboard, the original of which was made of Rosewood, illustrated in "Regency Furniture" by M. Jourdain. Circa 1820.
Top 10 x 46. Height 33.

No. 1106 Butler's Tray
Adapted from a butler's tray in the possession of Lord Ashton, England. Stationary Tray.
Top 22 x 30. Height 20.

No. 1433 Ivy Stand
A late 18th Century flower stand in the possession of John Pearson, London, England and reproduced by his permission. A similar model from Normanton Park, Rutland, is illustrated in MacQuoid's "Dictionary of English Furniture."
Width 17. Height 59.

No. 7086 Sofa
Reproduced from an original Hepplewhite model imported from England by a New York antique dealer and now in the Baker collection.
Width 76. Depth 30. Height 38.

Georgian Mahogany Group

No. 707 Chair
Typical English lounge chair.
Width 32. Height 36. Depth 34.
NOTE: Chair without ruffle No. 767.

No. 913 Sofa Table
Sheraton sofa table of the early 19th
Century. From the collection of Gill and
Reigate.
Top closed 27 x 36. Open 27 x 58.
Height 28.
NOTE: No. 1713 same table with yew tree
inlays — see page 20.

No. 902 Butler Tray
Adapted from an English butler's tray of the
late 18th Century. (Removable tray.)
Top open 26 x 34. Height 19.
Top folds as No. 900. See page 42.

No. 972 Table
Reproduced from a Chinese Chippendale
table now in the Cooper-Union Museum,
New York.
Top 20 x 20. Height 26.

No. 2943 Lamp Table
Adapted from a whatnot in the possession
of the Earl of Shaftesbury, St. Giles House,
England.
Top 13 x 17. Height 26.
NOTE: This piece can also be furnished
without gallery.

No. 1139 Desk
Reproduced from an antique model in the
Chicago Art Institute. Circa 1745. Leather
top.
Base 32 x 59. Height 30.
NOTE: Lower two right-hand drawers single
filing compartment.

No. 1418 Bookcase

Adapted from an 18th Century bookcase imported from England and now in a New York collection.

Top 11 x 33. Height 32.

No. 1428 Flower Table

Adapted from a Sheraton dressing table of the late 18th Century, illustrated in T. A. Strange's "English Furniture of the 18th Century." Circa 1795. Leather top.

Top 17 x 40. Height 26.

No. 1963 Dumb Waiter

Reproduced from a Chippendale dumb waiter sold at an antique sale by the American Art Association.

Upper top 20 x 20. Lower 26 x 26.
Height 33.

No. 900 Butler Tray

Adapted from an English butler's tray of the late 18th Century. (Removable tray.)
Top closed 18 x 27. Height 23.
NOTE: Top opens as No. 902. See page 41.

No. 951 Desk

Reproduction of an English Georgian desk, owned by Embury Palmer, reproduced by permission of the owner. Leather top.
Circa 1745.
Lower two right hand drawers single filing compartment.
Top 29 x 49. Height 30.

No. 760 Chair

Reproduced from a Sheraton chair, property of Judge John Cushing, and sold by the American Art Association.
Width 23. Depth 23. Height 34.

Georgian Mahogany Group

No. 1794
Breakfront Secretary Bookcase
Adapted from a Hepplewhite Breakfront
secretary bookcase imported from England
and recently sold at a New York antique
sale. Leather lined writing bed.
Width 56. Depth 15. Height 83.
NOTE: No. 1795 same piece of pine — see
page 26.

No. 6962 Lamp Table
Sheraton whatnot of the early 19th Century
in a private collection in New York.
Top 20 x 20. Height 30.
NOTE: No. 1160 same table. Top 15 x 20.
Height 30.

No. 1744 Coffee Table
Adapted from the base of an early 19th
Century chair, similar models of which are
illustrated by Duncan Phyfe. Leather top.
Top 30 x 30. Height 18.

No. 1718 Table
English circa 1785. Reproduced from an
original drop-leaf table from the Percival
Griffith's collection, London, England.
Top open 16 x 25. Closed 16 x 13.
Height 27.

No. 9028 Sofa
Length 76. Depth 36. Height 31.
No. 9033 — Same piece love seat size 52 in. long.
See page 49.

Georgian Mahogany Group

No. 9035 Sofa
A comfortable sofa of English style. A similar piece is owned by the Duke and Duchess of Windsor.

Length 84.   Depth 37.   Height 34.

NOTE: Piece also available without straight flounce as shown.

No. 192 Urn Table
Adapted from an English 18th Century urn table from a private collection shown at Messrs. Christie's, London, England. Leather top.

Top 12 x 16.   Height 27.

No. 1251 Console Bar
Reproduced from a mahogany drinking table, the property of Miss Tyndall, and illustrated in MacQuoid's "A History of English Furniture." Circa 1790.

Top 21 x 48.   Open 35 x 48.
Height 27.

NOTE: No. 1250 same piece coffee table height—see page 21.

No. 9014 Lounge Chair
Width 31.   Depth 37.   Height 32.

No. 1796 Secretary
Reproduced from a Sheraton secretary illustrated in the Connoisseur Magazine, in the possession of Owen Evans Thomas, England. Leather lined writing bed.
Interior writing compartment as No. 1786 — see page 50.

Width 36.   Depth 18.   Height 89.

NOTE: No. 1796½ same piece without pediment top.

NOTE: No. 1996 same piece with mirror door and without pediment. Photograph on request.

Georgian Mahogany Group

No. 6965½ Bookcase

Adapted from a Chippendale bookcase imported from England and now in a New York collection.

Top 11 x 33. Height 33.

NOTE: No. 6965 same piece without yew tree inlay.

No. 359 Wall Mirror

Reproduced from an antique mirror of the Hepplewhite School bought from John A. Pearson, an antique dealer in South Kensington, London, England. The original is now in our collection.

Finished Antique Pine, Antique Gold or Gold Leaf.

Plate 25 x 37. Height 58.

No. 914 Drum Table

Mahogany inlaid Sheraton drum table, circa 1790, found in Richmond, Virginia, and probably imported from England. Revolving leather top.

Top 32 x 32. Height 28.

NOTE: No. 1714 same table with yew tree inlays — see page 19.

No. 7036 Chair

Reproduced from a late Sheraton chair imported from England and now in the Baker collection.

Width 21. Depth 21. Height 34.

No. 921 Magazine Rack

English Canterbury of the early 19th Century, in the collection of Miss Ware, Belgrave Square, London.

Top 14 x 21. Height 19.

No. 704 Wing Chair

Similar to one in Essex Institute, Salem, Mass. Circa 1750.

Width 32. Height 46. Depth 30.

Georgian Mahogany Group

No. 702 Arm Chair
English 18th Century, illustrated in Lenygon's "Furniture in England," 1660 to 1760.
Width 26. Height 36. Depth 21.

No. 702½
Same Chair with Button Back.

No. 1515½ Breakfront Secretary Bookcase
Adapted from the center section of a large mahogany bookcase in five compartments from the board room of "English Country Life." Leather lined writing bed. Pine.
Base 16 x 60. Height 81.

NOTE: No. 1763 same piece in mahogany with yew tree inlays — see page 19.

No. 1952 Cocktail Table
The details of this table were reproduced from a directoire table desk in the collection of a Chicago antique dealer. Leather top.
Top closed 30 x 30. Top open 30 x 47. Height 18.
NOTE: No. 1952½ same piece with Parquet top — see page 48.

No. 1670½ Chest
Reproduced from an early Georgian chest in the possession of a New York antique dealer, and illustrated in the Connoisseur magazine. Walnut.
NOTE: No. 1670 chest same piece of mahogany — see page 82.

No. 9013 Lounge Chair
Width 31. Depth 38. Height 32.

No. 1125 Drum Table

Adapted from an English 18th Century book
table illustrated in MacQuoid's "Dictionary
of English Furniture." Leather top. Leather
book backs permanent part of table.

Top 34 x 34.   Height 30.

No. 7063 Bench

Reproduced from a Chippendale window
seat sold at the American Art Association
Galleries, New York.

Length 59.   Depth 16.   Height 27.

No. 357 Wall Mirror

Reproduced from a Chippendale mirror purchased from an antique dealer at Eagle
street in Red Lion Square, London, England,
and now in the Baker collection.
Finished Antique Pine, Antique Gold or
Gold Leaf.

Plate 16 x 26.   Height 44.

No. 1108 Nest of Tables

Copied from a set of tables in the possession
of Mrs. Stileman, London, England.
Leather top.

Top 15 x 26.   Height 25.

NOTE: No. 1708 same table with yew tree
top on largest table — see page 25.

No. 7074½ Sofa

Reproduced from a Chippendale settee in
the Cooper-Union Museum, New York.
Width 63.   Depth 25.   Height 36.

NOTE: No. 7074 same piece with tight seat.
Photograph on request.

No. 960 Chest

Reproduction of antique bachelor's chest in
the collection of Mrs. Frank Leonard, formerly owned by the Ackerman galleries.
Top closed 13 x 29.   Open 26 x 29.
Height 30.

NOTE: No. 1760 same piece with yew tree
inlay — see page 18.

Georgian Mahogany Group

No. 1784 Desk

Adapted from a desk owned by Owen Evans Thomas, at 20 Dover Street, London, England, and illustrated in the Connoisseur magazine. Leather top.

NOTE: Lower two right-hand drawers single filing compartment.

Top 24 x 42.   Height 30.

NOTE: No. 1783 same desk without inlay. Photograph on request.

No. 8068 Wing Chair

Reproduced from an early Georgian wing chair by permission of Frederic Tibbenham, Esq., of Ipswich, England.

Width 29.   Depth 32.   Height 42.

No. 1952½ Cocktail Table

The details of this table were reproduced from a directoire table desk in the collection of a Chicago antique dealer.   Parquet top.

Top closed 30 x 30.   Top open 30 x 47. Height 18.

NOTE: No. 1952 same table with leather top — see page 46.

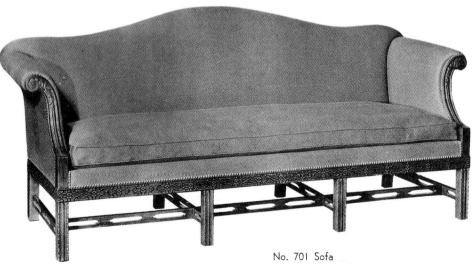

No. 2940 Commode

Adapted from a Chippendale table in the Metropolitan Museum, New York.

Top 12 x 18.   Height 26.

No. 701 Sofa

Chippendale, adapted from one illustrated by Cescinsky.   Circa 1750.

Length 88.   Height 35.   Depth 32.

Georgian Mahogany Group

No. 9033 Love Seat
A small sofa of modified Charles of London design.
Length 52. Depth 36. Height 33.

No. 1736 Corner Stand
Reproduced from a Sheraton corner wash-stand in the collection of Mrs. Heber Curtis. A similar piece is in the collection of Colonel Osburn, The Red House, Surrey, England.

Top 16 x 23. Height 32. Gallery 10.

NOTE: No. 1736½ same piece without gallery.

No. 1421 Spider Leg Table
Reproduced from the collection of the late Sir James Horlick is this interesting mahogany spider leg table. Circa 1765.
Top 21 x 29. Open 29 x 42.
Height 17.

No. 1411 Sofa Table Desk
A Sheraton mahogany writing table in the possession of an English antique dealer and illustrated in the Connoisseur Magazine. Circa 1800. Leather top.
Top 24 x 42. Desk Height 29.

No. 9040 Wing Chair
Width 34. Depth 33. Height 44.

Georgian Mahogany Group

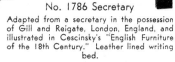

No. 283 Coffee Table
Adapted from a Sheraton urn stand in the
Baker collection. Leather top.
Top 21 x 28.   Height 17.
NOTE: No. 283½ same piece with wood top.

No. 6975 Chair
Copied from a Chippendale chair purchased
in England and now in the Baker collection.
Width 28.   Depth 28.   Height 38.

No. 946 Pembroke Table
Sheraton Pembroke table; from the collec-
tion of Mr. A. Hanney of England. Circa
1875.
Top closed 19 x 30.   Open 30 x 37.
Height 28.

No. 1786 Secretary
Adapted from a secretary in the possession
of Gill and Reigate, London, England, and
illustrated in Cescinsky's "English Furniture
of the 18th Century." Leather lined writing
bed.
Width 36.   Depth 18.   Height 88.
NOTE: No. 1786½ same piece without
pediment top.

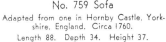

No. 759 Sofa
Adapted from one in Hornby Castle, York-
shire, England. Circa 1760.
Length 88.   Depth 34.   Height 37.

No. 2930 Lamp Table
Adapted from a small chest or end of the
early 18th Century from the Fermoye Collection, Grosvenor, England.
Top 13 x 18.   Height 26.

Georgian Mahogany Group

No. 1995 Desk

Adapted from an original Georgian Desk
owned by an American collector, similar
examples of which have been illustrated
by Chippendale in his book "The Gentleman
and Cabinet Maker's Directory" published
in 1754. Leather top.
Top 34 x 72. Height 30.
NOTE: No. 1990 same desk 34 x 60.
No. 1994 same desk 36 x 66.
Photographs on request.

No. 1487 Dumb Waiter

Reproduced by permission from a late 18th
Century dumb waiter in the collection of
Mrs. Van Leer Wills. Circa 1795.
Lower Shelf 24 x 24.
Top Shelf 19 x 19. Height 35.
NOTE: Support swings to hold leaves
horizontal.

No. 3537½ Cocktail Table

The details of this table were reproduced
from a Louis XV Fauttoir. Leather top.
NOTE: No. 3537 same table of beech with
marbelized top — see page 110.
NOTE: No. 3542½ same table — 21 x 30 —
see page 55.

No. 9007 Love Seat

Length 55. Depth 32. Height 30.

No. 7087 Chair

Reproduced from an original model imported
from England by a New York antique dealer.
Width 27. Depth 29. Height 34.

Georgian Mahogany Group

No. 7048½ Sofa
Reproduced by permission from an original Hepplewhite sofa belonging to George Blundell, English antique dealer.
Length 76. Depth 30. Height 35.
NOTE: No. 7048 sofa with tight seat.

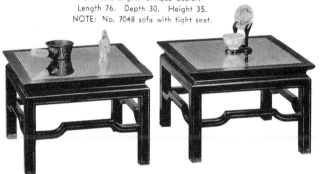

No. 1955½ Coffee Tables
Reproduced from a Chinese table in the collection of a Chicago antique dealer. Similar pieces are illustrated in "Chinese Furniture" published in London by Benn Brothers, Ltd. Mirror top. Black and gold or mahogany.
Top 20 x 20. Height 13.
NOTE: No. 1955 coffee table same piece with leather top.
NOTE: No. 1954 coffee table same piece — 17" high — see page 11.

No. 1461 Stand
Reproduced from a Mahogany Chippendale candle stand, the original of which was purchased in England and is now in the Baker collection.
Top 13 x 13. Height 47.

No. 973 Arm Chair
Reproduced from a Georgian chair recently acquired by the Metropolitan Museum, New York. Beech, natural or painted.
Width 26. Height 38. Depth 23.

No. 1879 Commode
Adapted from a Sheraton commode illustrated in T. A. Strange's "English Furniture during the 18th Century." Circa 1780.
Top 20 x 48. Height 34.

Georgian Mahogany Group

No. 1764 Secretary
Adapted from an early Georgian secretary imported from England and in a New York collection. Leather lined writing bed. Walnut.
Width 36. Depth 18. Height 81.

No. 9045 Lounge Chair
Width 32. Depth 39. Height 31.

No. 901 Butler Tray
Adapted from an English butler's tray of the late 18th Century. (Removable tray.)
Top 28 x 38 open. Height 19.
NOTE: Hinged top folds as No. 900 Butler's Tray, page 42.

No. 1719 Urn Table
Reproduced from an English 18th Century urn table, with an inlaid patera in the frieze, from a private collection shown at Messrs. Christie's, London, England. Circa 1770. Leather top. Pull-out candle slide.
Top 10 x 14. Height 27.
NOTE: 1719½ Table same piece with wood top.

No. 9003 Sofa
Adapted from a Chippendale sofa in the possession of Col. Sir John H. Ward and illustrated in the Connoisseur Magazine. Circa 1770.
Length 78. Depth 33. Height 35.

Georgian Mahogany Group

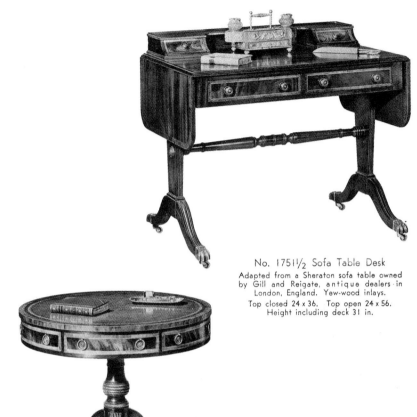

No. 7054 Wing Chair
Adapted from a Chippendale fireside chair illustrated in "The Collector's Guide."
Width 27. Depth 29. Height 41.

No. 1751½ Sofa Table Desk
Adapted from a Sheraton sofa table owned by Gill and Reigate, antique dealers in London, England. Yew-wood inlays.
Top closed 24 x 36. Top open 24 x 56.
Height including deck 31 in.

No. 1797 Drum Table
Adapted from an early 19th Century drum table illustrated in the Connoisseur Magazine. Leather top. Yew tree inlays.
Top 30 x 30. Height 27.

No. 9018 Chair
Width 27. Depth 29. Height 33.

No. 7076 Wing Chair
Copied from an unusual wing chair, the original of which is now in the collection of a Chicago antique dealer.
Width 38. Depth 32. Height 40.

No. 746 Chair
Reproduced from a Hepplewhite chair imported from England and now in the Baker collection. Beech.

Width 24.   Depth 24.   Height 37.

No. 1946 Pembroke Table
Reproduced from a Hepplewhite table purchased in England, and of which there are many similar models in his book, "The Cabinet Maker and Upholsterer's Guide," published in 1794. Yew tree inlays.

Top closed 30 x 19.   Top open 30 x 38.
Height 28.

No. 3542½ Coffee Table
The details of this table were reproduced from a Louis XV Fauttoir. Leather top.

Top 21 x 30.   Height 18.

NOTE: No. 3542 same table of beech with marbleized top — see page 112.

NOTE: No. 3537½ same table — 30 x 30 — see page 51.

No. 1766 Chest
Adapted from an English tall boy of the late 18th Century.

Base 16 x 23.   Height 48.

NOTE: No. 1966 same size piece with serpentine front.   Photograph on request.

No. 9036 Love Seat
Length 58.   Depth 36.   Height 34.

No. 9019 Chair
Adapted from a late Sheraton chair illustrated in Herbert E. Binstead's "English Chairs." Circa 1800.

Width 25.   Depth 26.   Height 35.

Regency Group

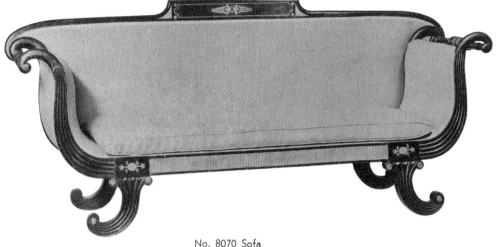

No. 8070 Sofa
Empire. Reproduced from an original model purchased from a California importer, and now in the Baker collection. Black and Gold.
Length 90. Depth 29. Height 37.

No. 1553 Cocktail Table
Adapted from an occasional table of the Regency period. Leather top. Mahogany or Black and Gold.
Top 20 x 34. Height 17.
(No. 1553½ same piece in Mahogany with brass trim.)

No. 1710 Stand
Reproduced from an antique carved Torchere showing the influence of Adam and found in collection of the Pelham Galleries, Chelsea, London, England. Gold Leaf, Antique Pine, or Black and Gold.
Top 11 x 11. Height 48.

No. 8079 Chair
Regency. Reproduced from an original chair in the Victoria and Albert Museum, South Kensington, London, England. Black and Gold.
Width 23. Depth 23. Height 33.

No. 1711 Stand
Reproduced from a 19th Century stand from the collection of a New York importer and now in the Baker collection. Black and Gold.
Top 14 x 17. Height 29

No. 1709 Commode
Reproduced from an original antique Regency Commode purchased from "Sheraton, Inc.", an antique dealer of Fulham Court Road, London, England, and now a part of the Baker collection. Black and Gold.
Top 9 x 35. Height 34.

Regency Group

No. 1701 Table

Regency. Reproduced from a 19th Century sewing table from the collection of "Sheraton, Inc.," an antique dealer of Fulham Court Road, London, England. This piece is now in the Baker collection. Black with Gold decoration.

Top 20 x 26. Height 28.

NOTE: Compartment below hinged top.

No. 8074 Bench

Reproduced from a late Sheraton piece found in an antique shop on lower Belgrade Street, London, England, and now a part of the Baker collection. Pickled beech or Black and Gold.

Top 13 x 36. Height 30.

No. 8081 Bench

English Regency. Reproduced from an original early 19th Century X bench from Decor, New York importers, and now in the Baker collection. Painted and decorated.

Top 14 x 23. Height 15½.

No. 1911 Coffee Table

The details of this table were reproduced from a 19th Century stand from the collection of a New York importer, and now in the Baker collection.

Black and Gold. Plate glass or marbleized top.

Top 30 x 30. Height 18.

No. 8073 Arm Chair

Regency. Reproduced from original 19th Century Regency arm chair purchased in England and now a part of the Manor House collection. Usually finished in Old Black and Gold.

Width 25. Depth 25. Height 35.

No. 1590 Commode

Reproduced from a Sheraton wing-front cabinet brought from England for the Baker collection. Yew-wood.

Top 12 x 42. Height 30.

Note: 1590½ Commode same piece in Mahogany with Yew-wood inlays.

Page 57

Regency Group

No. 1706 Table

Reproduced from an original 19th Century Regency stand purchased in England and now in the Baker collection. Black and Gold. Leather top.

Top 17 x 22. Height 27.

No. 1500 Chair

Reproduced from an original Regency arm chair purchased in England and now a part of the Baker collection. Black with Gold decoration.

Width 23. Depth 24. Height 37.

No. 8080 Arm Chair

Reproduced from an original Regency chair brought from England and purchased for the Baker collection from a New York importer. Old Black and Gold or Mahogany.

Width 23. Depth 28. Height 36.

NOTE: Side chair to match — see page 75.

No. 8015 Bench

Reproduced from an English regency bench from the collection of a New York importer.

Width 31. Depth 16. Height 23.
Seat Height 16.

No. 1446 Whatnot

Reproduced from an early 19th Century whatnot now in a New York collection. A similar model is illustrated in Jourdain's "Regency Furniture." Circa 1819.

Width 19. Depth 15. Height 55.

No. 1448 Drop Leaf Table

A late 18th Century drop leaf table reproduced by permission of the owner — an Eastern importer.

Top closed 21 x 34. Open 42 x 34.
Height 28.

Regency Group

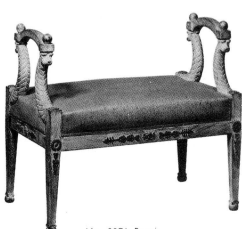

No. 8071 Stool
Reproduced from an early 19th Century rope stool of carved wood purchased from an antique dealer in Quay Dorsey, Paris, France. The original is now in the Baker collection. Antique Pine or Gold Leaf.
Width 28. Depth 28. Height 20.

No. 8076 Bench
Reproduced from an Empire bench purchased from an antique dealer in Euston Road, London, England, and now in the Baker collection. Brass Mounts. Beech.
Top 19 x 31. Height 27.

No. 1703 Candle Stand
Reproduced from a mahogany tripod candle stand purchased from Chalmers & Baxter, South Kensington, London, England and now in the Baker collection.
Top 12 x 12. Height 34.

No. 1702 Table
Reproduced from a Sheraton lyre base table purchased in England and now in the Baker collection.
Top 16 x 22. Height 28.

No. 8072 Chair
Reproduced from an unusual 19th Century chair found in the collection of an antique dealer in Berkeley Square, London, England, and now in the Baker collection. Paint and gold decoration.
Width 21. Depth 22. Height 33.

No. 1583½ Sofa Table
Reproduced from a late Sheraton sofa table purchased in England and now a part of the Baker collection. Yew tree inlays.
Top closed 24 x 38. Open 24 x 58.
Height 28.
NOTE: No. 1583 Sofa Table same piece in yew tree — photograph on request.

Regency Group

No. 1707 Stand
Reproduced from a Regency stand of unusually choice detail purchased from Decor, New York City, and now in the Baker collection. Black and Gold.
Top 18 x 18.   Height 25.

No. 7031 Chair
Reproduced from an English Regency chair purchased in England, and now in our collection. Similar model illustrated in Mac-Quoid's Dictionary. Natural beech or black and gold.
Width 22.   Depth 21.   Height 32.

No. 1861 Coffee Table
Adapted from an early 19th Century rope stool of carved wood purchased from an antique dealer in Quay Dorsey, Paris, France, the original of which is in the Baker collection. Antique Pine or Gold Leaf.
Top 28 x 28.   Height 16.

No. 1809 Cabinet
Reproduced from a late 18th Century break-front cabinet purchased in England and now in the Baker collection.
Base 12 x 42.   Height 72.

No. 1444 Chair
Reproduced from an early 19th Century elbow chair purchased in England and now a part of the Baker collection.
Mahogany or Painted.
Width 24.   Depth 24.   Height 35.

No. 1451 Chest
An unusual chest of the early 19th Century — the original of which is in the collection of a New York importer — and which was reproduced by permission.
Top 19 x 34.   Height 33.

Baker Dining Room Furniture, photographed by The James Bayne Company.

Dining Room Furniture
In the GEORGIAN Manner

There are more than a thousand carefully chosen patterns in the Baker Collection, none of which are of greater importance than this selection of dining room furniture. It is the largest collection of fine traditional reproductions for the dining room, available in this country.

In gathering together these designs, many of which are completely unique and outstanding in their artistic worth, consideration has been given to the demand for simpler style as well as for the more elaborate fashions. Also, these groups have been assembled with due thought for a variety of budgetary requirements.

Georgian Walnut Group No. 1899

No. 1899 Sideboard

Reproduced from a Georgian sideboard
made in 1770 by John Bradburn for Buckingham Palace under George III.

Width 78. Depth 24. Height 36.

NOTE: Four silver and three linen drawers
behind center doors.

No. 1899 Arm Chair

Reproduced from a Hepplewhite arm chair
in a private Eastern collection. Walnut or
mahogany.

Width 25. Depth 25. Height 37.

No. 1899 Server

Adapted from a walnut chest with drawers
illustrated in R. W. Symonds' "English Furniture." Circa 1755.

Width 40. Depth 20. Height 32.

NOTE: No. 1899½ server same piece in
mahogany.

Georgian Walnut Group No. 1899

No. 1899 Chair
Reproduced from a Hepplewhite arm chair in a private Eastern collection. Walnut or mahogany.

Width 23.   Depth 23.   Height 36.

No. 1899 Cabinet
Adapted from a pine "Kent" bookcase illustrated in British Art Magazine "Old Furniture." Available either in pine as shown or decorated. Photograph on request.

Width 68.   Depth 13.   Height 86.

No. 1899 Table
The details of this table were reproduced from an 18th Century side table in the Victoria and Albert Museum, London, England. Circa 1760-1765.

Top 48 x 70.   Height 30.
10-foot extension.

Georgian Mahogany Group No. 1889

No. 1889 Sideboard

Reproduced from a Georgian sideboard
made in 1770 by John Bradburn for Buckingham Palace under George III.

Width 78.   Depth 24.   Height 36.

NOTE: Four silver and three linen drawers
behind center doors.

No. 1889 Chair

Reproduced from an original antique model
purchased in England and now a part of the
Baker collection.

Width 22.   Depth 20.   Height 37.

No. 1889 Arm Chair

Reproduced from an original antique model
purchased in England and now a part of
the Baker collection.

Width 26.   Depth 25.   Height 37.

No. 1889 Server

Reproduced from a large half round commode in the possession of a New York
antique dealer.

Width 56.   Depth 24.   Height 36.

Georgian Mahogany Group No. 1889

No. 1899 Arm Chair
Reproduced from a Hepplewhite arm chair in a private Eastern collection. Walnut or mahogany.
Width 25. Depth 25. Height 37.

No. 1899 Chair
Reproduced from a Hepplewhite arm chair in a private Eastern collection. Walnut or mahogany.
Width 23. Depth 23. Height 36.

No. 1889 Cabinet
Adapted from a Sheraton breakfront bookcase illustrated in "English Furniture of the Georgian Period."
Width 67. Depth 13. Height 86.

No. 1889 Table
The details of this table were reproduced from an 18th Century side table in the Victoria and Albert Museum, London, England. Circa 1760-1765.
Top 48 x 70. Height 30.
10-foot extension.

No. 1879 Sideboard

A reproduction of a Hepplewhite mahogany inlaid sideboard, the property of L. Fleischmann, Esq., and illustrated in Percy MacQuoid's, "The History of English Furniture."

Top 28 x 78.   Height 42.

No. 1435 Chair

Hepplewhite chair with finely carved vase splat reproduced by permission from a private collection in Queen's Road, Dalston, England.

Width 21½.   Depth 17.   Height 37.

No. 1435 Arm Chair

Hepplewhite chair with finely carved vase splat reproduced by permission from a private collection in Queen's Road, Dalston, England.

Width 22   Depth 18.   Height 37½.

No. 1879 Server

Adapted from a Sheraton commode illustrated in T. A. Strange's "English Furniture During the 18th Century." Circa 1780.

Top 20 x 48.   Height 34.

No. 1890 Arm Chair

A Georgian ladder-back chair reproduced from an original model now in the Baker collection.

Width 24. Depth 24. Height 37.

NOTE: No. 1890½ same chair with spring seat.

No. 1890 Chair

A Georgian ladder-back chair reproduced from an original model now in the Baker collection.

Width 21. Depth 22. Height 36.

NOTE: No. 1890½ same chair with spring seat.

No. 1879 Cabinet

Sheraton. Reproduced from an inlaid mahogany cabinet, now in the possession of F. C. Hunter, Esq.

Width 51. Depth 16. Height 82.

No. 1879 Table

Reproduced from a Duncan Phyfe table from the collection of Dr. Reginald H. Sayre.

Top 50 x 72. Height 30.

10-foot extension.

No. 1249 Sideboard

Reproduced from a Sheraton sideboard in the possession of Mr. T. Seed, and illustrated in MacQuoid's "Dictionary of English Furniture." Circa 1785.
Top 26½ x 78. Height 36.

No. 1249 Chair

Reproduced from an original Hepplewhite chair purchased in England and now in the Baker collection. A similar model is illustrated in MacQuoid's "Age of Satinwood."
Width 21. Depth 23. Height 36.

No. 1249 Arm Chair

Reproduced from an original Hepplewhite chair purchased in England and now in the Baker collection. A similar model is illustrated in MacQuoid's "Age of Satinwood."
Width 25. Depth 24. Height 37.

No. 1249 Console

Reproduced from a Sheraton card table in the possession of Leicester Harmsworth, Bart, England. Circa 1780.
Top 20 x 46. Height 32.

No. 975 Arm Chair
Reproduced from an English 18th Century
chair in the Metropolitan Museum.
Width 24.   Height 39.   Depth 19½.

No. 1249 Cabinet
Reproduced from a Sheraton breakfront
cabinet in the Victoria and Albert Museum,
South Kensington, England. Circa 1780.
Base 14½ x 59.   Height 80.

No. 976 Chair
Reproduced from an English 18th Century
chair in the Metropolitan Museum.
Width 23.   Height 37.   Depth 19.

No. 1249 Table
Reproduced from an original English 18th
Century table illustrated in the Connoisseur
Magazine by an English antique dealer.
Top 48 x 88.   Height 29.   10-foot Extension.
NOTE: Three Pedestal Table is No. 1249½.
Closed 48 x 94.   12-foot Extension.

No. 1088 Sideboard

Reproduced from a Hepplewhite sideboard illustrated in T. A. Strange's "English Furniture of the 18th Century."

Top 26 x 80. Height 36.

NOTE: 1088½ same sideboard without inlays.

No. 599 Arm Chair

Hepplewhite, about 1790, from the collection of W. H. Erwing.

Width 24. Depth 22. Height 38.

No. 1084 Commode

English, 1790, adapted from one in the C. H. F. Kenderman collection, London, England.

Top 20 x 42. Height 33.

NOTE: No. 648 Commode same piece without inlay. Decorated No. 648½ — Write for Photograph.

No. 599 Chair

Hepplewhite, about 1790, from the collection of W. H. Erwing.

Width 21. Depth 20. Height 37.

No. 1436 Side Chair
A fine shield-back Hepplewhite chair with carved swag and Prince of Wales feathers reproduced by permission from a private collection in Queens Road, Dalston, England
Width 20½. Depth 21. Height 36½.

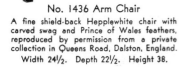

No. 1436 Arm Chair
A fine shield-back Hepplewhite chair with carved swag and Prince of Wales feathers, reproduced by permission from a private collection in Queens Road, Dalston, England.
Width 24½. Depth 22½. Height 38.

No. 1085 Cabinet
Adapted from a Sheraton bookcase at the "Treasure House," Preston, England.
Base 17 x 48. Height 80.

No. 1084 Table
Copied from an original of Sheraton design illustrated in "Arts and Decorations."
Top 46 x 72. 8-foot Extension.

18th Century Mahogany Group No. 1099

No. 1099 Sideboard
Reproduced from a Sheraton sideboard illustrated in the Connoisseur Magazine and in the possession of Frederick Treasure, Esquire, of Preston, England.
Top 28 x 78. Height 40.

No. 1441 Chair
Copied by permission from a Georgian chair, probably designed by Robert Manwaring, in a private collection in Queen's Road, Dalston, England.
Width 22. Depth 23. Height 38.

No. 1441 Arm Chair
Copied by permission from a Georgian chair, probably designed by Robert Manwaring, in a private collection in Queen's Road, Dalston, England.
Width 25. Depth 25. Height 40.

No. 1099 Commode
Reproduced from an 18th Century decorated commode in Buckingham Palace, London, England. Plain or decorated.
Top 20 x 55. Height 34.

No. 1099 Arm Chair

Reproduced from a Hepplewhite model imported from England and now in the Baker collection. Mahogany or Beech.

Width 23. Depth 22. Height 37.

No. 1099 Chair

Reproduced from a Hepplewhite model imported from England and now in the Baker collection. Mahogany or Beech.

Width 22. Depth 21. Height 37

No. 1099 Cabinet

Reproduced from an 18th Century secretary bookcase in the Victoria and Albert Museum, South Kensington, England. Top center drawer secretary desk with leather lined writing bed.

Base 18 x 52. Height 80.

No. 1099 Dining Table

Reproduced from an English Sheraton table recently imported and now in a private Eastern collection. Similar model illustrated in MacQuoid's "Dictionary of English Furniture."

Center section sold separately.

Center section open 48 x 62. Closed 48 x 22.
Console ends — Width 48. Depth 26.
Two 20-inch leaves.

No. 1539 Sideboard

A reproduction of a Hepplewhite sideboard owned by Blachard Randall, Esq. Yew-wood inlay.

Top 26 x 72. Height 36.

No. 1539 Chair

Reproduced from a model illustrated in William MacPherson Homer, Jr.'s "Philadelphia Furniture, 1682-1807."
Width 21. Depth 23. Height 37.

No. 1539 Arm Chair

Reproduced from a model illustrated in William MacPherson Homer, Jr.'s "Philadelphia Furniture, 1682-1807."
Width 25. Depth 24. Height 39.

No. 1539 Table

A dining table typical of the type made by Thomas Sheraton in England and in America by Duncan Phyfe during the early part of the !9th Century. Yew-wood inlay.
Top 46 x 68. Height 29.
10-f^ot Extension.

18th Century Mahogany Group No. 1539-1540

No. 1539 Server

Reproduced from a card table of Sheraton influence now in the Baker collection. A similar one is illustrated by Charles Over Cornelius in "Furniture Masterpieces." Yew-wood inlay.

Top closed 17 x 36. Open 34 x 36. Height 30.

No. 1539 Cabinet

This piece is adapted from a bookcase made to the order of one James Hunter, about 1780 by a "competent artificer." Yew-wood inlay

Base 14 x 42. Height 88.

(No. 1539½ Secretary — Top drawer secretary desk with leather lined writing bed.)

No. 1540 Sideboard

Adapted from the base of a Georgian breakfront bookcase in the collection of Mrs. H. Hope of London, England. Circa 1795. Yew-wood inlay.

Top 19 x 66. Height 36.

18th Century Mahogany Group No. 1549

No. 1549 Sideboard

Reproduced from an exceptionally fine piece in the collection of Mrs. Miles White. This sideboard is ornamented with shell and pendant husk inlays and Yew-wood cross-banding.

Top 26 x 74. Height 36.

No. 1549 Chair

Chippendale. Reproduced from an original antique model purchased from Bartholomew and Fletcher, Tottenham Court Road, London, and now in the Baker collection.

Width 21. Depth 22. Height 37

No. 1549 Arm Chair

Chippendale. Reproduced from an original antique model purchased from Bartholomew and Fletcher, Tottenham Court Road, London, and now in the Baker collection.

Width 25. Depth 24. Height 38.

No. 1892 Chest Server

Reproduced from a Hepplewhite chest of drawers in the collection of a Chicago antique dealer. Yew tree inlays. Pull-out tray under top.

Top 20 x 35. Height 35.

18th Century Mahogany Group No. 1549

No. 1289 Arm Chair

A particularly graceful example of a finely carved French Hepplewhite chair, reproduced by permission from a private collection in Queen's Road, Dalston, England. Width 24. Depth 23. Height 37.

No. 1289 Chair

A particularly graceful example of a finely carved French Hepplewhite chair, reproduced by permission from a private collection in Queen's Road, Dalston, England. Width 22. Depth 21. Height 36.

No. 1549 Cabinet

Adapted from a late Georgian wing front cabinet in an English collection. Circa 1795. Yew-wood inlays. Leather lined writing bed. Base 18 x 52. Height 81.

No. 1549 Dining Table

The four spindled pedestals ornamented with acanthus leaf carvings were introduced in America by Duncan Phyfe. Circa 1820. Yew-wood inlay. Top 48 x 72. Height 29. 10-foot Extension.

No. 1272 Sideboard
Adapted from a Regency sideboard of the
early 19th Century.
Top 26 x 72. Height 36.
NOTE: No. 1219 same sideboard without
inlay.

No. 1272 Arm Chair
Reproduced by permission from a late
Sheraton chair in a private collection in
Queens Road, Dalston, England.
Width 22. Depth 23. Height 35.

No. 1272 Server
Reproduced from the base of an original
Hepplewhite chest of drawers purchased in
London, England, for the Baker collection.
Circa 1775. Leather Lined Pull-Out Slide.
Top 20 x 33. Height 31.

NOTE: No. 1181 same piece without inlay.
See page 91.

No. 1272 Side Chair
Reproduced by permission from a late
Sheraton chair in a private collection in
Queens Road, Dalston, England.
Width 21. Depth 22. Height 34.

Sheraton Mahogany and Satinwood Group No. 1272=8080

No. 8080 Arm Chair
Reproduced from an original Regency chair
brought from England and purchased for the
Baker collection from a New York importer.
Old Black and Gold or Mahogany.
Width 23. Depth 28. Height 36.

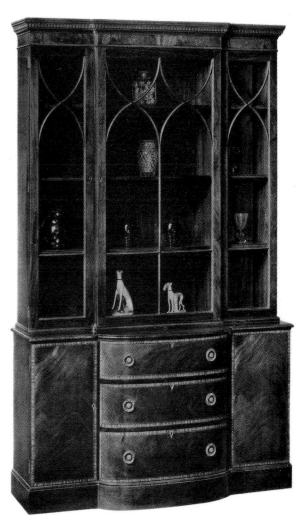

No. 8080 Chair
Reproduced from an original Regency chair
brought from England and purchased for the
Baker collection from a New York importer.
Old Black and Gold or Mahogany.
Width 19. Depth 25. Height 36.

No. 1272 Cabinet
Adapted from a Sheraton bookcase at "The
Treasure House," Preston, England.
Base 17 x 48. Height 80.

No. 1289 Table
Reproduced from a Sheraton table at "The
Treasure House," Preston, England. Yew-
wood inlays.
Top 48 x 88. 10-foot Extension.

No. 1080 Sideboard

English, end of the 18th Century, adapted from one in the collection of Sir William Plender, England.

Top 26 x 72. Height 36.

NOTE: Same Sideboard without inlay, No. 649

No. 1080 Chair

Reproduced from a Hepplewhite chair, the property of J. Rochelle Thomas, London.

Width 19½. Depth 20. Height 37.

No. 1080 Arm Chair

Reproduced from a Hepplewhite chair, the property of J. Rochelle Thomas, London.

Width 22½. Depth 22. Height 38.

No. 1080 Server

Adapted from an 18th Century dressing table, the property of George Dando, England.

Top 19 x 36. Height 32.

No. 789 Arm Chair

Reproduced from a Chippendale chair
purchased in England, and now in the
Baker collection. Similar model illus-
trated by Cescinsky in his book on
English furniture. Circa 1760.
Width 25. Height 37. Depth 20.

No. 789 Chair

Reproduced from a Chippendale chair
purchased in England, and now in the
Baker collection. Similar model illus-
trated by Cescinsky in his book on
English furniture. Circa 1760.
Width 22. Height 37. Depth 19.

No. 1080¹/₂ Cabinet

Sheraton, about 1800, from the collection
of Mrs. Percy MacQuoid, London, England.
Base 16 x 42. Height 78.
NOTE: No. 422 same cabinet without inlay.

No. 1080 Table

Reproduced from a Sheraton table owned
by Mr. I. Sack of Boston.
Top 44 x 68. 8-ft. Extension.

NOTE: Same table with plain top No. 649.
Three pedestal table No. 1087, without inlay
No. 659. Photographs on request.

No. 1669 Sideboard

Adapted from a Hepplewhite shaped front sideboard illustrated in Wenham's "The Collector's Guide to Furniture Designs." Yew-wood inlays.

Top 26 x 76.   Height 36.

No. 1669 Chair

Reproduced from an original antique model purchased in England and now a part of the Baker collection. This chair is an excellent example of that termed "Country Chippendale."

Width 21.   Depth 20.   Height 36.

No. 1669 Arm Chair

Reproduced from an original antique model purchased in England and now a part of the Baker collection. This chair is an excellent example of that termed "Country Chippendale."

Width 26.   Depth 22.   Height 37.

No. 1670 Chest Server

Reproduction of an early Georgian chest in the possession of a New York antique dealer, and illustrated in the Connoisseur Magazine. Mahogany.

Top 16 x 34.   Height 32.

NOTE: 1670½ same piece of walnut — see page 46.

No. 1012 Arm Chair
Reproduced from a Duncan Phyfe chair in
the Metropolitan Museum, New York.
Width 23.   Depth 23.   Height 36.

No. 1012 Chair
Reproduced from a Duncan Phyfe chair in
the Metropolitan Museum, New York.
Width 20.   Depth 21.   Height 34.

No. 1670 Cabinet
The details of this cabinet were copied from
a Hepplewhite escritoire bookcase illustrated in MacQuoid's "The Age of Satinwood" and the property of Robert Eastwood, Esq., England. Circa 1773. Boxwood
inlays.
Base 16 x 40.   Height 72.

No. 1669 Table
Adapted from an original English table in
a New York private collection. Yew-wood
inlays.
Top 44 x 66.   8-foot Extension.

No. 1679 Sideboard

Adapted from the base of a Georgian breakfront case in the collection of Mrs. H. Hope of London, England. Circa 1795. Yew-wood inlays.

Top 19 x 66. Height 36.

No. 1679 Arm Chair

Adapted from a Hepplewhite chair illustrated in Herbert E. Binstead's "English Chairs."

Width 24½. Depth 19. Height 39.

No. 1679 Chair

Adapted from a Hepplewhite chair illustrated in Herbert E. Binstead's "English Chairs."

Width 19½. Depth 17. Height 38.

No. 1822 Table

Adapted from a Hepplewhite dining table in the possession of Mr. Basil Oxendon and illustrated in MacQuoid's "Dictionary of English Furniture." Circa 1775. Yew tree inlays.

Top 46 x 70. Height 29¼. 8-foot Extension.

No. 1083 Arm Chair
Reproduced from an antique in a private English collection, which was sold by the American Art Association at an antique auction.

Width 24. Depth 23. Height 37.

No. 1083½ Same Chair upholstered over rail.

No. 1083 Chair
Reproduced from an antique in a private English collection, which was sold by the American Art Association at an antique auction.

Width 21. Depth 21. Height 36.

No. 1083½ — Same chair upholstered over rail.

No. 1679 Cabinet
The original of this piece is typical of the cabinets made through the last third of the 18th Century. Adapted from one in the South Kensington Museum, London, England. Circa 1780. Yew-wood inlays.

Base 14 x 48. Height 76.

No. 1679 Table
Reproduced from an early 19th Century table illustrated in The Connoisseur magazine. Yew-wood inlay.

Top 44 x 66. 8-foot Extension.

No. 1892 Sideboard

Adapted from the base of a late 18th Century breakfront bookcase. Yew tree inlays.
Top 19 x 66. Height 36.
NOTE: No. 1894 sideboard same piece without inlay.

No. 1892 Chair

Reproduced from an original chair of the Georgian period purchased in England and now in the Baker collection.
Width 21. Depth 20. Height 38.

No. 1892 Arm Chair

Reproduced from an original chair of the Georgian period purchased in England and now in the Baker collection.
Width 23. Depth 22. Height 39.

No. 1689 Table

Adapted from a Sheraton three-part table illustrated by L. V. Lockwood in "Colonial Furniture in America."
Center section open 50 x 75. Closed 50 x 29.
Console ends. Width 50. Depth 27½.
Height 30.
NOTE: Drawer in center section.

No. 1609 Arm Chair

Reproduced from a Hepplewhite chair imported from England and now in a private Detroit collection.

Width 24. Depth 22½. Height 37.

No. 1609 Chair

Reproduced from a Hepplewhite chair imported from England and now in a private Detroit collection.

Width 20. Depth 21. Height 36.

No. 1299 Corner Cabinet

Adapted from an English 18th Century corner cupboard illustrated by an Eastern collector in a sale of antiques.

Top 24 x 39. Height 80

NOTE: No. 1299½ same cabinet without inlay.

No. 1689 Table

Adapted from a Sheraton three-part table illustrated by L. V. Lockwood in "Colonial Furniture in America."

Center section open 50 x 75. Closed 50 x 29.
Console ends. Width 50. Depth 27½.
Height 30.

NOTE: Drawer in center section.

18th Century Mahogany Group No. 1092-1821

No. 1092 Sideboard

Adapted from the base of a Georgian breakfront bookcase in the collection of Mrs. H. Hope of London, England. Circa 1795.

Top 19 x 66. Height 36.

No. 114 Arm Chair

Reproduced from a Chippendale chair illustrated in Herbert Cescinsky's book, "English Furniture of the 18th Century," and now in the possession of Percival D. Griffiths, Esq., London, England. Circa 1760.

Width 24. Depth 24. Height 36.

No. 114 Chair

Reproduced from a Chippendale chair illustrated in Herbert Cescinsky's book, "English Furniture of the 18th Century," and now in the possession of Percival D. Griffiths, Esq., London, England. Circa 1760.

Width 21. Depth 22. Height 36.

No. 1092 Table

Reproduced from a Sheraton table at "The Treasure House," Preston, England. Boxwood inlay.

Top 44 x 68. 8-foot Extension.

No. 113 Arm Chair
Adapted from a Chippendale chair illustrated in Herbert E. Binstead's book, "English Chairs." Circa 1760.
Width 23.   Depth 26.   Height 37.

No. 113 Chair
Adapted from a Chippendale chair illustrated in Herbert E. Binstead's book, "English Chairs." Circa 1760.
Width 21.   Depth 23.   Height 36.

No. 1821 Cabinet
An adaptation of a late 18th Century bookcase, detailed from T. A. Strange's "Furniture, Woodwork and Decoration of the 18th Century."
Width 49.   Depth 14.   Height 76

No. 1821 Table
Adapted from a Hepplewhite dining table in the possession of Mr. Basil Oxendon and illustrated in MacQuoid's "Dictionary of English Furniture." Circa 1775.
Top 44 x 66.   Height 30.
8-foot extension.

18th Century Mahogany Group No. 422

No. 422 Sideboard
Reproduced with the exception of inlay from a Sheraton sideboard of the period of 1790, and similar to one made by Gillow of Lancaster.

Top 26 x 72.   Height 36.

No. 1894 Chair
Reproduced from a mahogany chair — the property of Mr. Humphrey Lee.

Width 19.   Depth 21.   Height 37.

No. 1894 Arm Chair
Reproduced from a mahogany chair — the property of Mr. Humphrey Lee.

Width 24.   Depth 23.   Height 38.

No. 422 Dining Table
Adapted from an original in a New York private collection.

Top 47 x 69.   Height 29.   8-foot Extension.

NOTE: 423 Table same piece with rectangular top 47 x 68.

18ᵗʰ Century Mahogany Group No. 422

No. 1087 Arm Chair
Reproduced from a Chippendale chair shown by Fermoye, Ltd., of London, England.
Width 27. Depth 24. Height 37.

No. 1181 Chest Server
Reproduced from the base on an original Hepplewhite chest of drawers purchased in London, England, and now in the Baker collection. Circa 1775.
Leather lined pull-out slide.
Top 21 x 33. Height 31.

No. 422 Cabinet
Sheraton, Circa 1800. From the collection of Mrs. Percy MacQuoid, London, England.
Base 16 x 42. Height 78.

No. 1689 Sideboard
Adapted from a Hepplewhite sideboard illustrated in T. A. Strange's "English Furniture during the 18th Century." A similar model is now in a private Eastern collection.
Top 25 x 72. Height 36.

No. 1087 Chair
Reproduced from a Chippendale chair shown by Fermoye, Ltd., of London, England.
Width 22. Depth 22. Height 37.

18th Century Mahogany Group No. 1809=1811

No. 1811 Sideboard

Reproduced with the exception of inlay from a Sheraton sideboard — the original of which was purchased in England and is now in our collection. A similar model is illustrated in "The London Cabinet Maker's Book of Prices."

Top 25 x 60.   Height 36.

NOTE: 1811½ same piece with yew tree inlays — photograph on request.

No. 1809 Chair

Sheraton. Reproduced from an original imported model purchased from a New York importer and now in the Baker collection.
Width 19.   Depth 20.   Height 33.

No. 1809 Arm Chair

Sheraton. Reproduced from an original imported model purchased from a New York importer and now in the Baker collection.
Width 20.   Depth 22.   Height 33.

No. 1491 Drop Leaf Extension Table

The base of this table was reproduced from an unusually large English 18th Century drum table, the original of which is in our Manor House collection.
Top closed 24 x 42.   Open 42 x 54.
Height 28.   8-foot Extension.

No. 1809 Cabinet

Reproduced from a late 18th Century breakfront cabinet purchased in England and now in the Baker collection.
Base 12 x 42.   Height 72.

No. 1810 Sideboard

Adapted from a Sheraton sideboard purchased in England and now in the Baker collection. A similar model is illustrated in "The London Cabinet Makers' Book of Prices."

Top 22 x 60.   Height 36.

No. 1810 Chair

Reproduced from an English Regency chair with cane seat and gold decoration purchased from Parker & Sons, Ltd., antique dealers in London, England. The original is now a part of the Baker collection.

Width 18.   Depth 20.   Height 32.

No. 1810 Arm Chair

Reproduced from an English Regency chair with cane seat and gold decoration purchased from Parker & Sons, Ltd., antique dealers in London, England. The original is now a part of the Baker collection.

Width 22.   Depth 22.   Height 32.

No. 1810 Corner Cabinet

Adapted from an 18th Century English corner cupboard imported for a private Eastern collection.

Top 10 x 30.   Height 75.

No. 1820 Table

Adapted from a Sheraton drum table of the late 18th Century. 8-foot extension. Yew-wood inlay.

Top 46 x 54.   Height 29.   8-foot Extension.
NOTE: Table equipped with hinged drop legs for support when table is extended.

18th Century Mahogany Group No. 1819

No. 1819 Sideboard

Adapted from an early 19th Century Regency commode. Mahogany or Black and Gold.

Top 13 x 50. Height 34½.

No. 1819 Chair

English Regency. Reproduced from an original chair purchased from an antique dealer in Brompton Road, London, England. These chairs are now in the Baker collection. Black and Gold.

Width 18. Depth 20. Height 32.

No. 1819 Table

Reproduced from a Regency sofa table from the collection of Lady Sackville and illustrated in M. Jourdain's "Regency Furniture, 1795-1820." 7-foot extension. Yew-wood inlay.

Top 46 x 46. Height 29.

No. 1819 Arm Chair

English Regency. Reproduced from an original pair purchased from an antique dealer in Brompton Road, London, England. These chairs are now in the Baker collection. Black and Gold.

Width 22½. Depth 23. Height 32.

No. 1819 Server

Reproduced from a decorated Regency work table purchased from "Sheraton, Inc.," an antique dealer of Fulham Court Road, London, England, and now in the Baker collection. Black and Gold.

Top closed 17 x 34. Top open 34 x 34. Height 30.

18th Century Mahogany Group No. 1822-1829

No. 1822 Sideboard
Reproduced from an "Oxford" sideboard in the collection of a New York antique dealer.

Top 52 x 17. Height 33.

No. 1829 Arm Chair
Reproduced from a Sheraton chair, purchased from an Eastern collector and now a part of the Baker collection.

Width 21. Depth 22. Height 32.

No. 1829 Table
Reproduced from a drop leaf table of the Sheraton school, the original of which is in a private Chicago collection.

Top closed 21 x 36. Top open 41 x 36.
Height 28½. 6-foot extension.

NOTE: Table equipped with hinged drop legs for support when extended.

No. 1829 Chair
Reproduced from a Sheraton chair, purchased from an Eastern collector and now a part of the Baker collection.

Width 20. Depth 21. Height 32.

No. 1810 Table
Reproduced from an original antique model in the possession of Mr. John Milton Quaintance.

Top 41 x 43. Height 29.
Extension 8 feet.

18th Century Mahogany Group

No. 1890 Chest Server

Adapted from a Georgian chest-with-drawers illustrated in R. W. Symond's book, "English Furniture from Charles II to George II." Circa 1755. Yew tree inlays.

Top 20 x 40. Height 32.

NOTE: No. 1890½ chest server same piece without inlay.

No. 1010 Chair

Reproduced from a Chippendale c purchased in England, and now in Baker collection. Similar model i trated in Cescinsky's "Book on Eng Furniture."

Width 24. Height 38. Depth 18.
Arm Chair to Match.

No. 1239 Cabinet

Reproduced from a Sheraton breakfront cabinet in the Victoria and Albert Museum, South Kensington, England. Circa 1780.

Base 14 x 58. Height 80.

No. 1011 Arm Chair

Reproduced from a Chippendale chair purchased in England and now in the Baker collection. Similar model illustrated in Cescinsky's "Book on English Furniture."

Width 24. Height 38. Depth 18.
Side Chair to Match.

No. 1540 Table

Reproduced from an original antique model in the Boston Museum of Fine Arts.

Top closed 46 x 77. Top open 46 x 115.
Center section closed 46 x 27.
Center section open 46 x 65.
End section 46 x 25.

NOTE: Table opens as No. 1689 — see page 87.

A Distinctive Bedroom Furnished with Baker Reproductions.

A Collection of
ENGLISH BEDROOM Furniture

"Suites of bedroom furniture were unknown in 18th Century England. In most instances, however, there was a relationship in the scale and general design of the pieces assembled for use in one room. Similar thought has been given to the selection of the various pieces for each group presented in the following pages. It will be noted that there is no monotonous repetition of detail within a group, yet all the pieces suggested for use in a single grouping bear harmonious relationship to each other.

For those who wish to create individuality in various room settings there is much material in this "bedroom" section

that is suitable for other uses. For instance, chests often make attractive serving pieces in the dining room or are quite at home in living room or hall; "night" tables can frequently be used as occasional pieces for the living room, and so forth.

As with all Baker furniture, everything has been done to preserve the feeling of authenticity in these bedroom pieces. Where designs are adaptations, as in the majority of beds, the requirements for modern living have been combined with traditional motifs.

No. 2989 Wall Mirror

Reproduced from a mirror of the Hepplewhite period in the possession of Robert Smith, Esq., and illustrated in Wallace Nutting's "Furniture Treasury." Circa 1775. Mahogany and Antique Gold.

Overall Size 52 x 28.   Plate 22 x 30.

No. 2979 Bench

Reproduced from a Hepplewhite bench illustrated in his book "The Cabinet Maker's and Upholsterer's Guide," published in 1794.
Width 14½.   Length 30.   Height 24.

No. 2989 Dresser Base

Copied from a Hepplewhite "Dressing Drawers" illustrated in the Apollo magazine.
Top 21 x 44.   Height 34.

No. 1172 Portable

Reproduced from a Sheraton portable mirror imported from England and now a part of the Baker collection. A similar model is illustrated in MacQuoid's "The Dictionary of English Furniture." Circa 1780.
Plate 13 x 17.   Height 23.

No. 2989 Night Table

Adapted from a small 18th Century Sheraton commode in the possession of Debenham & Freebody, London, England, and illustrated in the Connoisseur magazine.
Top 11 x 20.   Height 27.

No. 2989 Bed

Motifs copied from a chair illustrated in Hepplewhite's "The Cabinet Maker's and Upholsterer's Guide." Circa 1785. Twin or full size.
Headboard 40.   Footboard 27.

No. 2979 Chair

Reproduced from a Sheraton decorated arm chair imported from England and now in a private eastern collection. Circa 1800. Mahogany or painted and decorated.

Width 18. Depth 20. Height 31.

NOTE: Arm Chair to Match—see page 14.

No. 2989 Dressing Table Mirror

Reproduced from a Hepplewhite mirror illustrated in Nutting's "Furniture Treasury" and in the possession of an American collector. Gold Leaf or Antique Gold.

Overall Size 23 x 45.   Plate 18 x 28.

No. 2989 Dressing Table

Adapted from an 18th Century dressing table — a similar model of which is illustrated in MacQuoid's "Age of Satinwood." Leather top.

Top 20 x 46.   Height 30.

No. 2989½ Chest

Reproduced from a tall chest of drawers from the Adam School illustrated in Cescinsky's "English Furniture of the 18th Century" and in the possession of Percival D. Griffiths, Esq. Circa 1765-70.

Top 20 x 34.   Height 65.

No. 2990 Bed

Adapted from a bed designed by George Oakley, an English cabinetmaker, and in the possession of Mrs. Stileman, London, England. Twin or full size.

Headboard 38.   Footboard 26.

NOTE: No. 2943 same bed without upholstered headboard. See page 100.

No. 2943 Wall Mirror

Reproduced from a Sheraton mirror imported from England and now in the Baker collection. Antique Gold or Gold Leaf. Plate 20 x 34. Height 36.

No. 2943½ Powder Table

Adapted from a writing desk designed by Sheraton for Carlton House, London, England. Circa 1790. Leather top. Top 20 x 42. Height 31.

No. 2943 Dresser Base

Reproduced from a chest of drawers illustrated in Hepplewhite's "Cabinet Makers' and Upholsterers' Guide," published in 1794. Top 21 x 40. Height 35.

No. 2990 Bench

Adapted from an Empire X bench at Syon House, England. Circa 1785. Top 16 x 21. Height 19.

No. 2943 Arm Chair

Reproduced from original Regency chairs now in the Baker collection. Beech or paint. Width 21. Depth 20. Height 32.
NOTE: Side chair to match.
Width 20½. Depth 21. Height 31.

No. 2943 Bed

Adapted from a bed designed by George Oakley, an English cabinetmaker, in the possession of Mrs. Stileman, London, England.
Full or twin size. Height 38.
NOTE: No. 2990 Bed same piece with upholstered headboard. See page 99.

No. 2979 Dressing Table Mirror
Reproduced from a Hepplewhite mirror in the Sanderson collection and illustrated in Wallace Nutting's "Furniture Treasury." Circa 1790. Gold Leaf or Antique Gold. Overall Size 23 x 45. Plate 18 x 24.

No. 2943 Dressing Table
Adapted from a writing desk designed by Sheraton for Carlton House, London, England. Circa 1790. Leather Top. Top 20 x 42. Height 31.

No. 2943 Night Table
Adapted from a Sheraton whatnot in the possession of the Earl of Shaftesbury, St. Giles House, London.
Top 17 x 13. Height 26.
NOTE: This piece can also be furnished without gallery.

No. 2990½ Chest
Reproduced from an original Hepplewhite chest of drawers purchased in England and now in the Baker collection. Circa 1775. Leather lined slide. Satinwood inlays.
Base 20½ x 33. Height 54.
NOTE: No. 2979½ chest same piece without inlay.

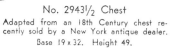

No. 2943½ Chest
Adapted from an 18th Century chest recently sold by a New York antique dealer. Base 19 x 32. Height 49.

No. 4459 Bed
Adapted from the motifs in a Sheraton "Drawing Room Chair" of the early 19th Century. Twin or Full Size. Headboard 42. Footboard 25.

No. 2931 Wall Mirror

Chippendale. Reproduced from an original model obtained from an antique dealer at Fitzroy street, London, England. This model is now in our collection.

Finished Antique Pine, Antique Gold or Gold Leaf.

Plate 17 x 28. Height 45.

No. 2930 Night Table

Adapted from a small chest or stand of the early 18th Century from the Termoil collection, Grosvenor, England.

Top 13 x 18. Height 26.

No. 2930 Dresser Base

Reproduction of a rare Chippendale chest in possession of a Regent Street, London, antique dealer and illustrated in the Connoisseur Magazine. Circa 1750.

Top 22 x 47. Height 33.

No. 2931 Bench

Copied from a Chinese Chippendale window seat. Circa 1760.

Top 16 x 24.

No. 2939 Chair

Reproduced from an antique chair purchased in Charleston, Virginia, and now in the Baker collection. Similar model illustrated in Wallace Nutting's book "Furniture Treasury."

Width 17. Depth 22. Height 34.

No. 2930 Bed

Adapted from a Chinese Chippendale bed in Cooper Union Museum, New York. Painted and Decorated or Mahogany.

Twin or full size. Height 45.

No. 2740 Dressing Table Mirror
Adapted from an 18th Century mirror in The Metropolitan Museum of Art, New York, and illustrated in E. G. Miller's "American Antique Furniture." Circa 1750-1775. Antique Gold.
Plate 20 x 26.   Overall 23 x 33.

No. 4459 Dresser Wall Mirror
Adapted from a late 18th Century mirror illustrated in Wallace Nutting's "Furniture Treasury." Antique Gold.
Plate 20 x 28.   Overall 25 x 40.

No. 2930 Dressing Table
Adapted from a Chippendale commode illustrated in MacQuoid's "Dictionary of English Furniture." Leather top.
Top 19 x 43.   Height 31.

No. 2930½ Chest
Adapted from Mahogany tallboy in the Percival Griffiths collection. Circa 1760.
Base 21 x 38.   Height 68.

No. 2940 Bed
Adapted from a Chippendale canopy bed illustrated in Cescinsky's book on English furniture.
Twin or Full Size.   Height 42.

No. 2730 Wall Mirror

Adapted from a late 18th Century Mahogany and Gold mirror from the collection of Mrs. W. W. Hubbard. Circa 1785. Mahogany and Gold.
Plate 20 x 30.   Overall 26 x 42.

No. 9025 Slipper Chair

Width 25.   Depth 29.   Height 29.

No. 2730 Dresser Base

Reproduced from a Chippendale chest in the Trangrove collection, Croyden, England.
Top 22 x 44.   Height 35½.

No. 2740 Bench

Adapted from a chair found at Sherborn, Mass., and belonging to the Harry W. Weeks collection.
Top 16 x 20.   Height 19.

No. 1969 Night Stand

Reproduction of a Chippendale commode from "Mersham Hatch," Kent, England, and made by Chippendale and Haig in 1769.
Top 15 x 18.   Height 27.
NOTE: 1970 same commode 23½ inches high.

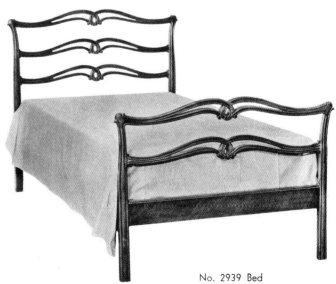

No. 2939 Bed

Details taken from a Hepplewhite ladder-back chair illustrated in Wallace Nutting's book "Furniture Treasury". Circa. 1760.
Twin or Full size.   Headboard Height 42.
Footboard Height 31.

No. 309 Bed

Adapted from a Chippendale chair purchased in England, and now in the Baker collection. Similar chair is illustrated in Herbert Cescinsky's book "English Furniture." Twin or Full Size.

Headboard height 42. Footboard height 33.

No. 2941 Chair

Copied from an original Sheraton chair now in the Baker collection. Natural Beech or Black and Gold.

Width 21. Depth 18. Height 33.

No. 2969½ Chest

Adapted from a Chippendale chest on chest illustrated in MacQuoid's "The Dictionary of English Furniture." Leather lined slide.

Base 19 x 36. Height 56.

No. 2931 Bed

Reproduced from a Chippendale bed in Cooper Union Museum, New York. Original model in Badmington House, England. Painted and Decorated or Mahogany. Twin or full size. Height 89.

No. 2740 Wall Mirror

Reproduced from an 18th Century mirror from the collection of John C. Toland and illustrated in E. G. Miller's "American Antique Furniture." Circa 1745. Antique Gold.

Plate 20 x 30. Overall 22 x 41.

No. 25 Chaise Longue

Adapted from a chair in Rufford Abbey, Nottinghamshire, England.
Width 28. Depth 40. Height 33.

No. 25 Stool

Width 28. Depth 19. Height 17.

No. 2740 Dresser Base

Chippendale. Adapted from a double chest at Bayfordbury, Herts, England, and illustrated in MacQuoid's "Dictionary of English Furniture."

Top 21½ x 44. Height 36.

No. 2740 Night Table

Adapted from a Chippendale table in the Metropolitan Museum, New York.
Top 12 x 18. Height 26.

No. 2740 Bed

Motifs for this bed were copied from a Chippendale canopy bed illustrated in Cescinsky's book on English Furniture. Twin or full size.
Headboard 47½.

No. 2740 Dressing Table Mirror

Adapted from an 18th Century mirror in The Metropolitan Museum of Art, New York, and illustrated in E. G. Miller's "American Antique Furniture." Circa 1750-1775. Antique Gold.

Plate 20 x 26.   Overall 23 x 33.

No. 2740 Chair

Reproduced from a chair found at Sherborn, Mass., and belonging to the Harry W. Weeks collection.

Width 18.   Depth 19.   Height 34.

No. 2740 Dressing Table

Adapted from a Georgian commode in Petworth, Sussex, and illustrated in MacQuoid's "Dictionary of English Furniture."

Top 20 x 42.   Height 30.

No. 2740 1/2 Chest

Adapted from a Chippendale Tallboy at Critchel, Dorset, England.

Top 19 x 37.   Height 51 1/2.

No. 2938 Canopy Bed

Reproduced from a Hepplewhite bed illustrated in Herbert Cescinsky's book "History of English Furniture."

Twin or full size.   Height 88.

18th Century Mahogany Group

No. 9051 Chair

Reproduced from an English lounging chair and stool.

Width 28. Depth 34. Height 36.

No. 9051 Stool

Width 18. Depth 26. Height 17.

No. 2990 Powder Table

Adapted from a late 18th Century Sheraton console formerly in the possession of an antique dealer in Brompton Road, London, England. Yew tree inlays.

Width 36. Depth 18½. Height 28½.

No. 2991 Standing Mirror

Adapted from an Italian baroque mirror of the late 18th Century. Antique Gold.

Overall Size 18 x 22. Plate 14 x 16.

No. 4479 Wall Mirror

Adapted from an early 18th Century mirror illustrated in Wienham's book "The Collector's Guide to Furniture Design." Mahogany and Antique Gold.

Plate 20 x 28. Overall 27 x 48.

No. 2992 Bed

The details of this bed were copied from the back of an early 19th Century sofa, a similar model of which is illustrated in "Colonial Furniture in America" by Luke Vincent Lockwood. Circa 1800-1810.

Width 78. Height 41.

NOTE: No. 2991 bed same piece without mirrored rail in headboard. Photograph on request.

Photograph taken in the Baker Showrooms, Grand Rapids, Michigan.

Reproductions In the FRENCH Manner

Few styles reflect the tastes and customs of their times more than the furniture of France in the late 18th Century. Nor is any style more adaptable to the homes of those who like a subtle, imaginative mode of decoration than the simpler examples of that period.

In adding to our collection of French Reproductions we have followed the course we established when our Fontainebleau group was introduced in the autumn of 1937. Choosing only the best pieces, obtaining them in most cases from sources not ordinarily accessible to furniture manufacturers, we have endeavored, in reproducing them, to retain all the nuances of form and color that are inherent in the originals.

Many of these recent additions have been reproduced from pieces in a collection of antiques purchased in France by Mr. Hollis S. Baker in anticipation of and just prior to France's entry into hostilities. Thus they represent some of the last authentic designs to come from that country.

These pieces are made from selected French walnut and beech and are finished in the best custom manner, by craftsmen who specialize in French finishes.

No. 3500 Sofa

Reproduced from a French transitional sofa
by permission of the owner — a private
collector.

Length 78. Depth 34. Height 32.

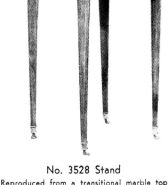

No. 3528 Stand

Reproduced from a transitional marble top
table imported from England and now in
the Baker collection. Leather lined candle
slides. Marbleized top.

Top 22 x 22. Height 28.

No. 3537 Cocktail Table

The details of this table were reproduced
from a Louis XV Fauttoir. Marbleized top.

Top 30 x 30. Height 18.

NOTE: No. 3537½ · same piece in mahog·
any with leather top. See page 51.

No. 3501 Wing Chair

Reproduced from a Bergere a Joues of the
Louis XVI period.

Width 29. Depth 33. Height 42.

No. 3548 Stand

Reproduced from a French gueridon at
Chantilly, Musée Condé, and illustrated in
Seymour de Ricci's "Louis XVI Furniture."

Top 16 x 16. Height 28.

No. 3504 Chair

Reproduced from a Louis XVI arm chair
formerly in the possession of a New York
importer and now in the Baker collection.

Width 23. Depth 22. Height 35.

No. 3541 Desk

Reproduced from a directoire table desk in the collection of a Chicago antique dealer. Leather top. Brass trimming. Walnut or Mahogany.

Top 28 x 52. Height 29.

No. 3505 Chair

An unusual Louis XVI arm chair found in the south of France and now in the Baker collection.

Width 24. Depth 23. Height 33.

No. 3523 Table

A directoire table reproduced from one from a private collection in Baden Baden, the original of which is now in the Baker collection.

Top 18 x 18. Height 30.

No. 3514 Chair

Reproduced from a Louis XVI arm chair imported from France and now in the Baker collection. A similar model is illustrated in Paul Avril's "L'Ameublement Parisien."

Width 24. Depth 30. Height 36.

No. 3521 Refraichissoir

Reproduced from a Louis XV Fruitwood refraichissoir found in Falaise, Calvados province, France, and now in the Baker collection. Synthetic marble top around flower wells.

Top 18 x 20. Height 28.

No. 3518 Chair
Reproduced from a pair of transitional chairs in the collection of a southern connoisseur.
Width 19. Depth 23. Height 34.

No. 3542 Coffee Table
The details of this table were reproduced from a Louis XV fauttoir. Marbleized top.
Top 18 x 30. Height 18.
NOTE: No. 3542½ same piece in mahogany with leather top. See page 55.

No. 3508 Chair
A Louis XV arm chair of unusual size purchased in Paris for reproduction, and now in the Baker collection.
Width 23. Depth 24. Height 32.

No. 3531 Commode
A transitional piece from the Normandy section of France. Reproduced from the original which is now in the Baker collection.
Top 14 x 21. Height 29.

No. 3534 Lamp Stand
Reproduced from a Directoire candle stand purchased in France and now in the Baker collection.
Height 35.

No. 3533 Hanging Cabinet
From a typical provincial Estagnier bought in Avignon in the south of France, and now in the Baker collection.
Width 30. Height 45.

No. 3559 Desk

Reproduced from an early 19th Century
desk purchased in France and now in the
possession of Helen Barnes Von Schrenck,
Pinehurst, North Carolina. Leather lined
writing bed folds out to open. Walnut or
Mahogany.

Base 15 x 29. Height 48.

No. 3555 Love Seat

Adapted from a French transitional sofa by
permission of the owner—a private collector.
Length 50. Depth 32. Height 32.

No. 1850 Chair

Reproduced from an original pair of antique
chairs purchased in France and now in the
Baker collection.

Width 19. Depth 21. Height 36.

No. 3549 Coffee Table

Adapted from a small table at Schloss
Robertsau, Alsace, France. Leather top.
Top 28 x 28. Height 17.

No. 961 Table

Reproduction of an Italian imported game
table. Circa 1760. Leather top.
Top 26 x 26. Height 29.

No. 3545 Table

Adapted from a "Table de Nuit" illustrated
in "Petit Mobilier." Walnut, Mahogany or
Rosewood.
Top closed 22 x 36. Open 22 x 58.
Height 28.

French 18th Century Group

No. 3530 Trumeau
Louis XVI. Reproduced from one found in France and now in the Baker collection. Paint and Gold.
Mirror 30 x 70. Plate 21 x 36.

No. 3512 Chair
Regency — early 19th Century. Reproduced from a pair made in London about 1815 and now in the Baker collection. Antique Black with Gold decoration.
Width 19. Depth 19. Height 34.

No. 3538 Lamp Table
Reproduced from a Louis XV stand in the collection of a New York antique dealer.
Top 20 x 20. Height 26.

No. 3524 Commode
Reproduced from a directoire Walnut commode found in Montpellier, Herault province, France, and now in the Baker collection.
Top 23 x 50. Height 33.
NOTE: Available with marble or wood top.

No. 3511 Chair
Reproduced from a Louis XV Fauttoir from an antique shop in Rue Jacob, Paris, France and now in the Baker collection.
Width 26. Depth 28. Height 36.

No. 3948 Commode
Reproduced from a Louis XVI stand in a New York antique collection. A similar model is in the collection of M. l'abbé Pinck, Cure de Hambach, Moselle, France. Marbleized top.
Top 12 x 18. Height 29.

No. 3536 Bookcase
Reproduced from a refined pair of Louis XVI open bookcases with brass gallery, purchased at a sale in the Anderson Galleries, New York, and now in the Baker collection.
Base 10 x 30. Height 40.

French 18ᵗʰ Century Group

No. 3510 Chair
Reproduced from a Louis XVI Bergere imported from the Normandie section of France and now in the Baker collection.
Width 31. Depth 31. Height 37.

No. 3535 Refraichissior
Reproduced from a Louis XV Fruitwood refraichissior purchased from a count's collection in Paris, and now in the Baker collection.
Top 16 x 16. Height 27.

No. 3515 Chair
Reproduced from a Louis XVI arm chair imported from France and now in the Baker collection. A similar model is illustrated in Paul Avril's "L'Ameublement Parisien."
Width 23. Depth 24. Height 34.

No. 3507 Chair
Reproduced from an original chair imported from France and now in the Baker collection.
Width 23. Depth 22. Height 33.

No. 3526 Desk
A Louis XV desk from the French province of Normandy. Reproduced from the original now in the Baker collection. Leather top.
Top 24 x 56. Height 30.
Note: 3598 same desk. Top 26 x 48.

No. 3595 Sofa

Reproduced from an antique French Provincial sofa in the possession of a Chicago antique dealer.

Width 75.   Depth 33.   Height 36.

No. 3582 Lamp Table

Adapted from a petite table in a private collection at Marevil-sur-lay, France. Leather top.

Top 18 x 26.   Height 27.

No. 3581 Cocktail Table

The details of this table were reproduced from a French table in the possession of a New York importer. Leather top.

Top 28 x 28.   Height 17.

No. 3586 Commode

Provincial. Reproduced from an original now in the Baker collection.

Top 11 x 18.   Height 27.

No. 3561 Whatnot Flower Stand

Reproduced from an Empire Rafraichi, purchased from Theo Meignerm, an antique dealer in Paris, France, and now in the Baker collection.

Top 15 x 18.   Height 30.

No. 3509 Chair

Reproduced from a Louis XV chair imported from France by a New York collector and now in the Baker collection.

Width 22.   Depth 27.   Height 45.

No. 3588 Commode

Reproduced from a Louis XV commode in the possession of the New York Historical Society.

Top 12 x 21½. Height 28.

No. 8075 Chair

A Louis XVI Bergere, the original of which was purchased from Theodore Meignen, an antiquaire in Rue du Cherché-mide, Paris, France, for the Baker collection.

Width 29. Depth 30. Height 38.

No. 3589 Lamp Table

Louis XV. Reproduced from a small table in the collection of a New York importer.

Top 14 x 21. Height 27.

No. 3593 Hanging Cabinet

Reproduced from a Venetian hanging cabinet of the first part of the 18th Century from the Cora Storrs Clark collection.

Width 16. Height 29.

No. 3597 Chair

Adapted from a Provincial arm chair illustrated in Charles Sadonl's "Le Mobilier Lorraine — Ensembles et Details," and belonging to Mme. Olivier of Nancy, France.

Width 25. Depth 24. Height 35.

No. 3591 Table Desk

The original of this Louis XV table desk is in the possession of a New York antique dealer. Leather top. Leather lined pull-out slides.

Top 22 x 36. Height 29.

French 18th Century Group

No. 3590 Desk
Reproduced from a Louis XV desk imported from France and now in the possession of a New York antique dealer. Leather top.
Top 23 x 33. Height 38.

No. 3576 Commode
Reproduced from an original provincial stand imported from France and now in the Baker collection.
Top 12 x 16. Height 28.

No. 337 Chair
Reproduced from an original purchased from the Lavezzo collection.
Width 24. Height 36. Depth 22.

No. 3516 Chair
Reproduced from a Louis XV Fauttoir purchased from a New York importer and now in the Baker collection.
Width 26. Depth 27. Height 37.

No. 3585 Stand
Reproduced from a stand illustrated in M. Paul Auril's book "Pendant la Revolution."
Top 13 x 19. Height 27.

No. 3580 Chest
The original from which this Louis XV chest was reproduced is in the Baker collection.
Top 16 x 28. Height 32.

French 18th Century Group

No. 3556 Chair
The details of this chair were reproduced from a French Louis XV sofa by permission of the owner — a private collector.
Width 27. Depth 27. Height 35.

No. 3584 Breakfront Bookcase
Reproduced except for size from a Louis XVI vitrine bought from a private collection near Cannes, French Riviera, France, and now in the Baker collection.
Top 16 x 54. Height 62.

No. 3592 Coffee Table
The details of this table were reproduced from a French table in the possession of a New York importer. Leather top.
Top 20 x 28. Height 17.

No. 3947 Commode
Reproduced from an original stand in the collection of a New York antique dealer.
Top 15 x 18. Height 29.

No. 3596 Chair
The details of this chair were copied from an antique provincial sofa from the collection of a Chicago antique dealer.
Width 28. Depth 30. Height 37.

No. 3587 Stand
French Empire. Reproduced from an original stand in the collection of a New York importer.
Top 13 x 19. Height 28.

No. 3650 Sideboard
Reproduced from an 18th Century French
buffet in the Museum of Historic Lorraine at
Nancy, France.
Width 76. Depth 20. Height 36.

No. 3550 Chair
Transitional Louis XV — Louis XVI. Reproduced from an extraordinary fine chair purchased from a count's collection in Paris —
but propably made in Italy.
Chairs made with spring seat.
Width 21. Depth 24. Height 36.

No. 3550 Arm Chair
Transitional Louis XV — Louis XVI. Reproduced from an extraordinary fine chair purchased from a count's collection in Paris —
but probably made in Italy.
Chairs made with spring seat.
Width 25. Depth 24. Height 40.

No. 3650 Server
Reproduced from a French chest imported
by a New York antique dealer.
Top 20 x 45. Height 33.

No. 3650 Arm Chair

Adapted from a Louis XV chair imported from France and now in the Baker collection. Chairs made with spring seat.

Width 24.   Depth 24.   Height 38.

No. 3650 Cabinet

Reproduced from a Louis XVI Vitrine bought from a private collection near Cannes, French Riviera, France, and now in the Baker collection.

Width 67.   Depth 16.   Height 68.

No. 3650 Table

Reproduced from a dining table found in a chateau in Rouen province, Normandy, France, and now in the Baker collection.

Top 46 x 70.   Height 30.
10-foot extension.

No. 3650 Chair

Adapted from a Louis XV chair imported from France and now in the Baker collection. Chairs made with spring seat.

Width 21.   Depth 22.   Height 38.

No. 3950 Sideboard

Reproduced from an original Traite illus
trated by Charles Moreau of Paris in a
typical French interior.

Top 19 x 66.   Height 37.

No. 3950 Chair

Reproduced from a provincial arm chair
illustrated in Charles Sadonl's "Le Mobilier
Lorrain—Ensembles et Dètails," and belonging to Mme. Olivier of Nancy, France.

Width 18.   Depth 21.   Height 36.

No. 3950 Arm Chair

Reproduced from a provincial arm chair
illustrated in Charles Sadonl's "Le Mobilier
Lorrain — Ensembles et Dètails," and belonging to Mme. Olivier of Nancy, France.

Width 22.   Depth 23.   Height 37.

No. 3950 Server

Reproduced from a transitional side table
in the possession of an Eastern importer of
antiques. A similar model is illustrated in
"Les Beaux Meubles Rustiques" by Docteur
J. Jambon.

Top 22 x 42.   Height 31.

No. 2950 Arm Chair
Reproduced from a French chair of the late 18th Century, illustrated by M. Paul Auril in his book "French Furniture Before, During and After the Revolution."
Width 23. Depth 24. Height 34.

No. 2950 Chair
Reproduced from a French chair of the late 18th Century, illustrated by M. Paul Auril in his book "French Furniture Before, During and After the Revolution."
Width 17. Depth 20. Height 34.

No. 3950 Cabinet
Adapted from a French Louis XV buffet in a private American collection. A similar model is illustrated in "Les Beaux Meubles Rustiques du Vieux Pays de Rennes" by Docteur J. Jambon.
Base 15 x 38. Height 75.

No. 3950 Table
Reproduced from a French provincial draw top table in the collection of a New York importer. A similar model is in the possession of M. P. Croctaine, Garenne, Lorain, France.
Top closed 42 x 64. Top open 42 x 104.
Height 30.

No. 2960 Arm Chair
Reproduced from a French chair of the late
18th Century illustrated by M. Paul Auril in
his book, "French Furniture Before, During,
and After the Revolution."
Width 22. Depth 24. Height 33.

No. 2960½ Welsh Dresser
Reproduced from a French provincial buffet
belonging to Madame Flandois of Nantes,
France, and illustrated in "Le Mobilier
Vendeen" by J. Ganthier
Top 20 x 58. Height 77.

No. 2960 Sideboard
Without Welsh dresser top.
Top 20 x 58. Height 35.

No. 2960 Chair
Reproduced from a French chair of the late
18th Century illustrated by M. Paul Auril in
his book, "French Furniture Before, During,
and After the Revolution."
Width 17. Depth 19. Height 33.

No. 2960 Server
Adapted from an original Provincial writing
table imported from France and now in the
Baker collection.
Top 22 x 43. Height 29.

No. 1849 Arm Chair

Reproduced from an original antique model in the style of Louis XVI purchased from Fields and Ford, New York importers. A similar model is illustrated in "L'AMEUBLE-MENT PARISIAN avant, pendant, et après LA REVOLUTION" by Paul Auril.

Width 22. Depth 23. Height 37.

No. 1849 Chair

Reproduced from an original antique model in the style of Louis XVI purchased from Fields and Ford, New York importers. A similar model is illustrated in "L'AMEUBLE-MENT PARISIAN avant, pendant, et après LA REVOLUTION" by Paul Auril.

Width 18. Depth 21. Height 36.

No. 2960 Cabinet

Adapted from a Louis XV Ponnetiere Maconnaisse from the collection of M. Morel-Poulachon, Tournus, France, and illustrated in the book, "Le Mobilier Bourguignon," by G. Jeanton.

Width 47. Depth 17. Height 60.

No. 2960 Table

Reproduced from an early 18th Century French table in the possession of M. P. Croctaine, Garenne, Lorain, France.

Top closed 38 x 60. Height 30.

Top open 38 x 96.

French Provincial Group No. 1849=1850

No. 1849 Sideboard

Reproduced from an unusual sideboard purchased from Raoul De La Foret Divonne, a member of the French nobility and a well known antique dealer in Paris. This piece shows the sturdy proportions of the country work of the Louis XVI period.

Top 17 x 58.   Height 38.

No. 1849 Chair

Reproduced from an original antique model in the style of Louis XVI purchased from Fields and Ford, New York importers. A similar model is illustrated in "L'AMEUBLEMENT PARISIAN avant, pendant, et après LA REVOLUTION" by Paul Auril.

Width 18.   Depth 21.   Height 36.

No. 1849 Arm Chair

Reproduced from an original antique model in the style of Louis XVI purchased from Fields and Ford, New York importers. A similar model is illustrated in "L'AMEUBLEMENT PARISIAN avant, pendant, et après LA REVOLUTION" by Paul Auril.

Width 22.   Depth 23.   Height 37.

No. 1850 Commode

Reproduced from a middle 18th Century commode purchased in France from Raoul De La Foret Divonne, an antique dealer in Paris. The original was apparently painted and decorated in the early 19th Century — and is now a part of the Baker collection. Plain or Decorated.

Top 18 x 38.   Height 31.

No. 1849 Cabinet

Reproduced from a country piece of the Louis XVI period, purchased from Raoul De La Foret Divonne, an antique dealer in Paris, France, and now in the Baker collection.

Width 53.   Depth 13.   Height 48.

No. 1849 Server

Reproduced from an original bow front commode purchased from an antique dealer at 27, Rue de Varenne, Paris, France, and now in the Baker collection.

Width 35.   Depth 14.   Height 33.

No. 1849 Table

Adapted from a Louis XV table in the possession of M. P. Croctaine, Garenne, Lorain, France.

Top 46 x 54.   Height 29.   8-foot Extension.

French 18th Century Group No. 3575=3576

No. 3575 Wall Mirror
An unusual Louis XV gold mirror dating about 1790, and now in the Baker collection. Gold leaf or antique gold.
Plate 22 x 32. Mirror 27 x 47.

No. 3575 Chair
Louis XVI slipper chair. The original, now in the Baker collection, was imported from France and sold at a recent New York antique auction.
Width 21. Depth 21. Height 32.

No. 3575 Dresser Base
A Louis XV commode dating between 1750-1770, definitely a country piece, and from Midi, south of France. The original is now in the Baker collection.
Top 25 x 48. Height 33.

No. 3575 Bench
Directoire. From an original bench, probably of Italian origin, now in the Baker collection.
Width 23. Depth 16. Height 19.

No. 3575 Night Table
Provencial. Reproduced from an original now in tne Baker collection.
Top 11 x 18. Height 27.

No. 3575 Bed
Directoire. The simplicity of this piece is typical of the period, and the original is in our collection. Twin or full size.
Width 40. Height 44.

No. 3786 Powder Table

Reproduced from a French tulipwood inlay powder table of the late 18th Century purchased from Ann Elsey Ruseau, an antique dealer in Paris, France, and now a part of the Baker collection. The original is an unusually rare piece and particularly valuable because it is signed by the maker, Sauvageon, one of the most famous cabinet-makers of the period.

Top closed 18 x 34. Top open 18 x 53.
Height 28.

Note: This photograph was taken of antique model.

No. 3576 Bench

Copied from an Empire bench for which a Roman Curule chair was the model.
Top 18½ x 15¼. Height 18.

No. 3575½ Chest

Reproduced from an original Louis XVI tall chest purchased from a New York importer and now in the Baker collection.
Base 17 x 31. Height 58.

No. 3576 Night Table

Reproduced from an original provincial stand imported from France and now in the Baker collection.
Top 12 x 16. Height 28.

No. 3576 Bed

Louis XV provincial. Reproduced from one imported from France and now in the Baker collection. A similar model is illustrated in Guillaume Janneau's "Lits de Repos & Lits." Twin or full size.
Headboard height 41. Footboard height 13.
Width 43.

No. 3787 Wall Mirror

Adapted from a French Trumeau purchased from a New York antique dealer and now in the Baker collection.

Overall size 29 x 42.   Plate 26 x 32.

No. 3786 Chair

Reproduced from an original chair purchased from the Count R. de la Roc collection in Paris, France. This piece is now in the Baker collection.

Width 18.   Depth 18.   Height 25.

No. 3785 Bench

English Regency. Reproduced from an original early 19th Century X bench from Decor, New York importers, and now in the Baker collection. Painted and decorated.

Top 15 x 22.   Height 16.

No. 3787 Dresser Base

Reproduced from an original antique French chest purchased in France and now in the Baker collection.

Width 49.   Depth 22.   Height 34.

No. 2946 Dressing Table Mirror

Adapted from an original Louis XV antique mirror in the Baker collection. Antique Gold.

Overall size 24 x 38.   Plate 18 x 24.

No. 2944 Night Stand

Directoire. Copied from a Acojon Petite commode, recently sold at an antique auction in New York.

Top 13 x 18.   Height 28.

No. 2945 Dressing Table

Adapted from a table in a French collection, illustrated by De Ricci. Leather top.

Top 20 x 44.   Height 30.

No. 2947 Dresser Mirror
Copied from an original French 18th Century mirror in the collection of a New York importer. Antique White and Gold.
Plate 20 x 26. Height 49.

No. 2945 Dresser Base
Reproduced from an imported French Directoire chest, circa 1790, in an Eastern collection.
Top 20 x 46. Height 33.

No. 3575 Dressing Table Mirror
Transitional. Purchased in London but probably made in France about 1800. The original is in our collection. Gold leaf or antique gold.
Plate 20 x 28. Mirror 25 x 43.

No. 2945½ Chest
Reproduced from an imported French chest, circa 1790, in an Eastern collection.
Base 17 x 33. Height 54.

No. 2945 Night Table
Reproduced from a "Table De Nuit" illustrated in "Petit Mobilier."
Top 13 x 20. Height 27

No. 2946 Bed
Details of this bed taken from an Italian 18th Century chair.
Twin or full size. Height 39.

No. 3947½ Wall Mirror

Reproduced from an imported French mirror
now in the Baker collection. Antique Gold.
Overall size 27 x 46.   Plate 22 x 30.

No. 3947 Night Table

Reproduced from an original stand in the
collection of a New York antique dealer.
Top 15 x 18.   Height 28.

No. 3947 Dresser Base

Reproduced from a French provincial chest
of drawers purchased in France and now a
part of the Baker collection.
Top 22 x 48.   Height 33.
NOTE: No. 3949 dresser same piece without carved drawer fronts.

No. 3947 Bench

Adapted from the base of an original
antique model in the style of Louis XVI
purchased from Fields and Ford, New York
importers. A similar model is illustrated in
"L'Amenblement Parisian avant, pendant et
aprés la Revolution" by Paul Auril.
Top 15 x 22.   Height 17.

No. 3947 Bed

Adapted from a Provincial bed in the col-
lection of Madam Flandrois at Nantes,
France.
Twin or full size.
Headboard height 43.   Footboard height 29.

No. 3947½ Dressing Table Mirror

The details of this mirror were adapted from an imported French mirror now in the Baker collection. Antique Gold.

Overall size 24 x 37.   Plate 18 x 26.

No. 3947 Chair

Reproduced from an original antique model in the style of Louis XVI purchased from Fields and Ford, New York importers. A similar model is illustrated in "L'Amenblement Parisien avant, pendant, et aprés la Revolution" by Paul Auril.

Width 18.   Depth 21.   Height 35.

(Note: Arm Chair to match—see page 125.)

No. 3947 Dressing Table

Reproduced from a Louis XV dressing table in the possession of a New York importer of antiques.

Top 19 x 36.   Height 29.

No. 3947½ Chest

Reproduced from an original antique model imported by a New York dealer and now in a private collection.

Top 17 x 31.   Height 56.

No. 3947½ Bed

Adapted from a Provincial bed in the collection of Madam Flandrois at Nantes, France.

Twin or full size.

Headboard height 43.   Footboard height 25.

French 18th Century Group No. 3948

No. 3948 Wall Mirror
Reproduced from a Louis XVI mirror purchased from Benson and Glick, New York antique dealers and now in the Baker collection. Antique Gold.
Overall size 25 x 49.   Plate 22 x 32.

No. 3948 Chair
Reproduced from a French chair of the late 18th Century. Illustrated by M. Paul Auril in his book "L'Amenblement Parisien avant, pendant, et aprés La Revolution."
Width 17.   Depth 20.   Height 34.
(Note: Arm Chair to match—see page 124.)

No. 3948 Dresser Base
Reproduced from an original provincial chest in the possession of Fields and Ford, New York antique dealers.
Top 20 x 45.   Height 33.

No. 3948 Bench
Reproduced from an original French provincial bench in the Baker collection.
Top 17 x 26.   Height 17.

No. 3948 Bed
Reproduced from an original bed imported from France by a New York antique dealer.
Twin or full size.
Headboard height 45.   Footboard height 29.

No. 3949 Dressing Table Mirror

Adapted from an original Louis XV antique mirror in the Baker collection. Antique Gold.
Overall size 24 x 38. Plate 18 x 24.

No. 3948 Night Table

Reproduced from a Louis XVI stand in a New York antique collection. A similar model is in the collection of M. l'abbé Pinck, Curé de Hambach, Moselle, France. Marbleized top.
Top 12 x 18. Height 28.

No. 3948 Dressing Table

Adapted from an imported French side table now in the Baker collection. Leather top.
Top 21 x 43. Height 29.

No. 3948½ Chest

Reproduced from a Provincial chest of drawers in an American collection of antiques.
Top 17 x 32. Height 50.

No. 3948½ Bed

Reproduced from an original bed imported from France by a New York antique dealer.
Twin or full size.
Headboard height 45.

Contract Work

Entrance to the Office of the Chairman, Federal Reserve Bank,
Atlanta, Georgia; which is furnished with Baker Furniture.

YOU will find Baker Furniture, Inc., always ready to cooperate in the planning and estimating of your contract work, whether for college, clubs, hotels, banks, public institutions or any projects in which careful selection and variety of types are important.

Such resources as the thousand active patterns in the regular Baker lines; the contract models we frequently have available, but which are not shown in our catalog; and our special order facilities, provide for a broad diversity of budgets.

Reproduced from an original shop front at 9 Norton Forgate, Algote, London, England.

Milling Road Shop

A DIVISION OF BAKER FURNITURE. Inc.

IN which a selection of 18th Century English furniture of authentic design, made with good materials, sound cabinet work and finish is offered at moderate prices.

The quality of Milling Road Shop* Furniture is that characteristic of all Baker furniture, but certain economies in production are effected through elimination of some of the handwork in cabinet making, finish and the choice of simpler models, and because of larger cuttings.

In these respects it is not as fine as our Connoisseur Furniture at higher prices, but we believe that Milling Road Shop Furniture is superior in design, workmanship and finish, to any other furniture offered at similar prices.

*Reg. U. S. Pat. Off.
Milling Road Shop Furniture is manufactured in Canada by Hespeler Furniture Co., Hespeler, Ontario.

No. 9014 Lounge Chair
Width 31. Depth 37. Height 32.

No. M858 Extension Cocktail Table
The details of this table were copied from a Sheraton sofa table in the possession of Lady Assleton Smith, London, England. Leather Top.

NOTE: Leather lined tray is stored in apron of table when closed.

Top closed 22 x 40. Top open 22 x 58. Height 17.

No. M855 Nest of Tables
The details of these tables were adopted from a late 18th Century stand in the Robert Stanford collection, Brighton, England. Leather top on largest table.

Top 18 x 22. Height 24.

No. M858 Extension Cocktail Table
The details of this table were copied from a Sheraton sofa table in the possession of Lady Assleton Smith, London, England. Leather Top.

NOTE: Leather lined tray is stored in apron of table when closed.

Top closed 22 x 40. Top open 22 x 58. Height 17.

No. M850 Breakfront Secretary Bookcase
The details of this breakfront cabinet were copied from an original bookcase found in New England and now in the Baker collection. Leather lined writing bed.

Width 55. Depth 16. Height 82.

No. 9020 Chair

Adapted from a Chippendale chair illustrated in Herbert Cescinsky's book on English Furniture. Circa 1760.

Width 26. Depth 31. Height 36.

No. M651 Sofa Table

Reproduced from a Duncan Phyfe sofa table illustrated in Charles Over Cornelius' "Furniture Masterpieces of Duncan Phyfe." Boxwood inlays.

Top closed 24 x 36. Open 24 x 55. Height 29.

Note: No. M654 Sofa Table same piece with leather top.

No. M862 Cocktail Table

Reproduced from a Chinese table in the collection of a Chicago antique dealer. Similar pieces are illustrated in "Chinese Furniture" published in London by Benn Brothers, Ltd. Leather top.

Top 30 x 30. Height 14½.

No. M683 Dumb Waiter

Adapted from a Sheraton two-tiered dumb waiter illustrated in T. A. Strange's "Eighteenth Century Furniture, Woodwork and Decorations."

Upper Shelf 15½ x 21. Lower Shelf 22 x 28. Height 26.

No. 9004 Sofa

A typical English Tuxedo sofa.

Length 77. Depth 33. Height 30.

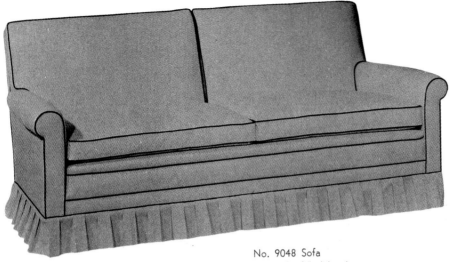

No. 9048 Sofa
A comfortable sofa of English style.
Length 76. Depth 36. Height 33.

No. M668 Whatnot
The details of this whatnot were copied
from an original American washstand from
the collection of Mrs. E. W. Merrifield illustrated in a book on early American stencils
by Janet Waring.
Top 20 x 20. Height 28.
NOTE: No. M669 Whatnot same piece with
top 15 x 20.

No. M657 Cocktail Table
Adapted from a Mahogany sofa table in
the Metropolitan Museum of Art and illus-
trated in "American Antique Furniture" by
Edgar G. Miller, Jr. Leather top.
Top closed 21 x 35. Open 21 x 50.
Height 17.

No. M53 Wing Chair
Adapted from an original English wing chair
now in the Cooper Union Museum, New
York. (Covered in imported English linen.)
Width 28. Depth 29. Height 40.

No. M483 Pedestal Table
Reproduced from an English original in the
Baker collection which type of table was
known as a "kettle stand." Circa 1790.
Top 16 x 16. Height 21.

No. M695 Secretary
Adapted from a Chippendale secretary
made for Horace Walpole at Strawberry Hill
by Gillows, London, England. Leather-lined
writing bed.
Width 36. Depth 18. Height 81.

No. M439 Lamp Table
Reproduced from a Sheraton whatnot in the Rixon collection at "Ye Olde Retreate," Dunstable, England.
Top 13 x 16. Height 26.

No. 9024 Wing Chair
Adapted from a wing chair in the possession of Mr. I. Sack, Boston, Mass. Circa 1750.
Width 34. Depth 29. Height 38.

No. M672 Bookcase
Adapted from a small Sheraton commode-bookcase brought from England for the Baker collection. Boxwood inlay. Mirror back in upper section.
Base 13 x 21. Height 48.

No. M864 Coffee Tables
The details of these tables were copied from a side table imported from China and in the possession of O. Roche, Esq., France. Black and Gold. Leather tops.
Top 20 x 20. Height 17.

No. M458 Chest
Adapted from a chest of drawers illustrated in Hepplewhite's "Cabinet Makers' and Upholsterers' Guide," published in 1794. Mahogany with Yew-wood banding.
Top 18 x 28. Height 30½.

No. M42 Love Seat
Reproduced from a Chippendale love seat sold at Christy's Galleries, London, England. Circa 1730.
Length 59. Depth 33. Height 34.

No. M675 Stand

Adapted from an early 19th Century stand from the collection of a New York importer and now in the Baker collection. Leather top.

Top 15 x 15. Height 17.

NOTE: No. M675½ Stand same piece with mirror top.

No. M660 Lamp Table

Adapted from a Sheraton urn stand in the Baker collection. Leather top.

Top 19 x 24. Height 26.

No. 9009 Wing Chair

Reproduced from an 18th Century wing chair, a similar one of which is in Essex Institute, Salem, Mass.

Width 32. Depth 32. Height 46.

No. M190 Coffee Table

Adapted from an occasional table of Sheraton style in the possession of a New York antique dealer. Leather top.

Top 24 x 32. Height 20.

No. M688 Whatnot

An adaptation of an early 19th Century whatnot in the Baker collection. A similar one is illustrated by M. Jourdain in "Regency Furniture."

Top 15 x 22. Height including gallery 29. Gallery 3 in.

No. M652 Drum Table

Adapted from an early 19th Century table illustrated in the Connoisseur Magazine. Leather top. Boxwood inlays.

Top 30 x 30. Height 27.

No. M467 Pie Crust Table
This Chippendale pie crust table is adapted from a table in the H. Blairman collection, Harrogate, England.
Top 29 x 29. Height 27.

No. 9032 Wing Chair
Adapted from an English wing chair now in the Cooper Union Museum, New York.
Width 30. Depth 30. Height 36.

No. M680 Tea Table
Adapted from an inlaid Rosewood sofa table from the collection of Messrs. Harris, London antique dealers. Circa 1800. Pull out candle slide.
Top 17 x 30. Height 23.

No. M191 Coffee Table
Adapted from a Sheraton two-tiered dumb waiter illustrated in T. A. Strange's "Eighteenth Century Furniture, Woodwork and Decorations." Leather top.
Top 22 x 28. Height 18.

No. M684 Whatnot
Adapted from an early 19th Century whatnot in the collection of the Earl of Shaftesbury.
Top 20 x 20. Height 27.
NOTE: No. M682 Whatnot same piece with top 15 x 20.

No. M658 Chest
Adapted from a chest of drawers illustrated in Hepplewhite's "Cabinet Maker's and Upholsterer's Guide," published in 1794.
Top 14 x 27. Height including gallery 35.
NOTE: No. M658½ Chest same piece without gallery. Height 29.

No. M10 Sofa

Chippendale, English 18th Century. Reproduced from one sold at a New York antique sale by the American Art Association.
Length 78.   Depth 33.   Height 35.

No. M656 Pembroke Table

Reproduced from a Hepplewhite table purchased in England, and of which there are many similar models in his book "The Cabinet Maker's and Upholsterer's Guide," published in 1794.   Boxwood inlays.
Top closed 18 x 26.   Open 34 x 26.
Height 29.

No. M662 Coffee Table

Adapted from a late 18th Century Sheraton drum table, the original of which was sold at auction by the American Art Association in New York. Leather top. 2 pull out candle slides.
Top 28 x 28.   Height 17.

No. M660½ Table

Adapted from a Sheraton urn stand in the Baker collection.   Leather top.
Top 18 x 18.   Height 26.

No. M555 Wig Stand

A typical wig stand of the 18th Century, similar to one in the Miles White collection.
Pedestal Spread 19.   Height 34½.

No. M55 Wing Chair

Adapted from a wing chair in the possession of Mr. I. Sack, Boston. A similar model is illustrated in MacQuoid's "Dictionary of English Furniture." Circa 1749. (Covered in imported English linen.)
Width 30.   Depth 31.   Height 40.

No. 9011 Chair
Adapted from a typical English lounge chair.
Width 27. Depth 36. Height 35.

No. M51 Desk Chair
Adapted from a Sheraton chair of the early 19th Century.
Width 22. Depth 25. Height 35.

No. M657½ Cocktail Table
Adapted from a Mahogany sofa table in the Metropolitan Museum of Art and illustrated in "American Antique Furniture" by Edgar G. Miller, Jr. Leather top
Top 21 x 39. Height 17.

No. M686 Pedestal Table
Adapted from a Chippendale piecrust table in the H. Blairman collection, Harrogate, England.
Top 30 x 30. Height 27.
NOTE: No. M687 same piece with serpentine shaped top — photograph on request.

No. M653 Desk
Reproduced from small secretary desk illustrated in Edgar G. Miller, Jr.'s, "American Antique Furniture" and in the collection of Mrs. Francis T. Redwood. Circa 1790-1810. Boxwood inlays. Leather lined writing bed folds forward to open. Size opened 28 x 36.
Base 19 x 36. Height 44.

No. M65 Sofa
Adapted from a sofa in a Belgrave Square
home, London, England.
Length 76. Depth 35. Height 31.

No. M156 Nest of Tables
Reproduced from a Sheraton nest of tables
belonging to Andrew Meikle, Chelsea, London. Leather top on largest table.
Top 12 x 21. Height 25.

No. M480 Tea Table
Adapted from a small rosewood table illus-
trated by M. Jourdain in his book on
Regency furniture. In the style of 1800.
Candle slides both ends.
Top 17 x 30. Height 24.

No. M64 Chair
Reproduced from a typical English type
club chair.
Width 27. Depth 35. Height 33.

No. M570 Stand
An adaptation of an English urn table of
the Sheraton school. Circa 1785.
Top 15 x 15. Height including gallery 25.

No. M452 Drum Table
Adapted from a Sheraton table at "Treasure
House," Preston, England. Mahogany with
Yew-wood banding. Leather top.
Top 30 x 30. Height 27.

No. M261 Drum Table
Reproduced from a table in the Hope collection of London. Circa 1810. Leather top.
Top 38 x 38. Height 29.

No. M445 Stand
Adapted from an original stand in the collection of E. Marshall-Hale, Esq.
Top 13 x 16. Height 26.

No. M464 Chair
Reproduced from a later Sheraton chair purchased in England and now in the Baker collection. Circa 1810. Mahogany or painted and decorated.
Width 18½. Depth 19½. Height 32.

No. M863 Cocktail Table
Reproduced from a Chinese table in the collection of a Chicago antique dealer. Similar pieces are illustrated in "Chinese Furniture" published in London by Benn Brothers, Ltd. Leather top.
Top 22 x 40. Height 14½.

No. M476 Desk — Back View

No. M12 Arm Chair
Reproduced from the original Judge Cushing chair in the old Boston State House. It is said to be the chair in which Judge Cushing sat when presiding at the trial of the British soldiers in the Boston Massacre. Circa 1780.
Width 24. Depth 22. Height 32.

No. M476 Desk — Front View
Adapted from a late 18th Century oval desk of the Sheraton school. Leather top.
Top 32 x 48. Height 30.
(Interior of each end accommodates stationery, etc.)

No. 9012 Lounge Chair
Width 32.   Depth 35.   Height 32.
No. 9029 Chair—Same chair with tight back.

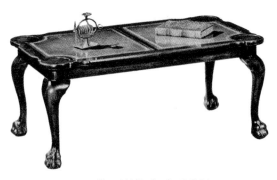

No. M665 Cocktail Table
Adapted from a Chippendale card table
illustrated in MacQuoid's "Dictionary of
English Furniture." Leather top.
Top 21 x 36.   Height 15.

No. M671 Coffee Table
Adapted from a Sheraton candle stand illus-
trated in the Connoisseur Magazine by a
London antique dealer. Leather top. 2 pull
out candle slides.
Top 28 x 28.   Height 17.

No. M663 Dumb Waiter
Reproduced by permission from a late 18th
Century dumb waiter in the collection of
Mrs. Van Leer Wills. Circa 1795.
Upper Shelf 16 x 16.   Lower shelf 21 x 21.
Height 31.

No. M650 Breakfront Secretary Bookcase
Reproduced from a Hepplewhite breakfront
secretary bookcase imported from England
and sold recently at a New York antique
sale. Boxwood inlays. Leather lined writing
bed.
Base 15 x 56.   Height 82.

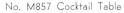

No. M460 Lamp Table

Adapted from an English 18th Century
table, circa 1745, illustrated in "The Collectors' Guide" by Edward Wenham.
Leather top.
Top 17 x 22. Height 27.

No. M60 Sofa

Adapted from an early 19th Century sofa
which was typical of the Grecian influence
in line, popular at that time.
Available both right and left.
Width 60. Depth 32. Height 33.

No. M857 Cocktail Table

Adapted from a sofa table of the Sheraton
period illustrated by T. A. Strange in his
book "The History of 18th Century Furniture." Leather top.
Top closed 22 x 37. Top open 22 x 52.
Height 17.

No. M853 Desk

Adapted from a Chippendale desk in the
possession of Lord Ebury, London, England.
Leather top. Boxwood and marquetry inlays.
Top 26 x 44. Height 30.

No. M70 Host Chair

An adaptation of an 18th Century "Grand-
mother's Chair."
Width 25. Depth 25. Height 44.

No. M50 Sofa

Adapted from an English 18th Century sofa
sold at a New York antique sale of the
American Art Association.

Length 77. Depth 32. Height 35.

No. M860 Lamp Table

Adapted from a late 18th Century table in
the Robert Stanford collection, Brighton,
England. Leather top.

Top 22 x 22   Height 26

No. M281 Drop-Leaf Cocktail Table

Adapted from a sofa table of the Sheraton
Period illustrated by Strange in his book
"History of 18th Century Furniture."
Leather top.

Top closed 21 x 36. Open 21 x 52.
Height 17.

No. M52 Chair

Adapted from a late Sheraton chair illustrated in Herbert E. Binstead's "English
Chairs." Circa 1800.

Width 24. Depth 27. Height 34½.

No. M582 Whatnot Stand

An adaptation of an early 19th Century
whatnot in the Baker collection. Similar
to the one illustrated by M. Jourdain in
"Regency Furniture."

Top 13 x 16. Height including gallery 28.

No. M69 Chair

Adapted from the original Judge Cushing
chair in the Old Boston State House.

Width 22½. Depth 24. Height 34.

No. M16 Love Seat

Adapted from one in a London interior,
illustrated in Connoisseur Magazine.
Length 55. Depth 33. Height 33.

No. M554 Tea Table

An English tea table with serpentine top
and fretted corner brackets, in the manner
of Hepplewhite. Circa 1785. Leather top.
Cupped Candle Slide.
Top 20 x 30. Height 25¼.

No. M861 Coffee Table

Adopted from a Chinese Chippendale table
in the Cooper Union Museum, New York.
Leather top. Antique black with gold
decoration.
Top 23½ x 30½. Height 19½.

No. M872 Bookcase

Adapted from a late 18th Century open
face bookcase at Denston Hall, England.
Mirror back.
Width 26. Depth 12. Height 50.

No. M851½ Sofa Table

Adopted from an original sofa table owned
by Gill and Reigate, London, England.
Leather top.
NOTE: No. M851 same table with wood
top.
Top closed 22 x 37. Top open 22 x 58.
Height 28.

No. M829 Wall Mirror

Reproduced from original model from the
collection of an Eastern importer.
Antique gold
Overall size 31 x 37.   Plate 24 x 28.

No. M829 Dresser Base

Reproduced from a Hepplewhite four-
drawer chest illustrated in Apollo Magazine.
Top 22 x 44.   Height 34.

No. M829 Night Table

Reproduced from an early 19th Century
table recently sold at a New York antique
sale.
Top 13 x 18.   Height 27.

No. M829 Bench

Motifs taken from an Empire X bench at
Lyon House, England. Circa 1785.
Top 21 x 16.   Height 18.

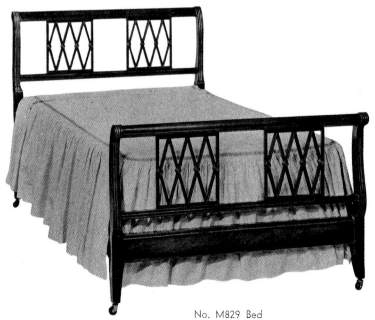

No. M829 Bed

The details of this bed were copied from a
late Sheraton chair in a private collection
in Queen's Road, Dalston, England.
Headboard 39.   Footboard 27.
Twin or Full Size.

No. M829 Dressing Table Mirror
Adapted from an early 19th Century mirror illustrated in Wallace Nutting's "Furniture Treasury." Circa 1810-1820. Antique gold. Overall size 24 x 32. Plate 18 x 30.

No. M829 Dressing Table
Adapted from an original sofa table owned by Gill and Reigate, London, England. Top closed 22 x 37. Top open 22 x 58. Height 28.
NOTE: No. M829½ same table with leather top.

No. M840 Mirror
The motifs of this mirror were copied from a Chinese table in the possession of Charles Vignier, Esq. Antique gold or mahogany. Overall size 27½ x 35. Plate 20 x 28.

No. M829 Chair
Adapted from a late Sheraton chair imported from England and now in the Baker collection. A similar model is illustrated in MacQuoid's "Dictionary of English Furniture." Width 18. Depth 20. Height 32.

No. M829½ Chest
Adapted from a tall chest of drawers illustrated in Cescinsky's "English Furniture of the 18th Century" and in the possession of Percival D. Griffiths, Esq. Circa 1765-1770. Top 19 x 36. Height 50.

No. M839 Wall Mirror

The details of this mirror were copied from
a Sheraton chair of the late 18th Century.
Antique white and gold or mahogany.
Overall size 26 x 39.   Plate 22 x 30.

No. M839 Night Table

Adapted from a Sheraton stand of the late
18th Century.   Antique white with gold
decorations or mahogany.
Width 18.   Depth 15.   Height 29.

No. M839 Dresser Base

Adapted from a Sheraton chest illustrated
in his book "The Cabinet Maker and Upholsterer's Drawing Book," published in 1802.
Top 21 x 44.   Height, including Gallery, 36.

No. M839 Bench

Adapted from the base of a Sheraton chair
in the Victoria and Albert Museum. Circa
1795. Antique white or antique black and
gold or mahogany.
Top 16 x 24.   Height 17.

No. M839 Bed

The details of this bed were copied from a
Sheraton chair in the Victoria and Albert
Museum, London, England.   Antique white
with gold decoration or mahogany.
Headboard 38.   Footboard 14.
Twin or Full Size.

No. M839 Dressing Table Mirror

Adapted from a late 18th Century dressing glass illustrated in Wallace Nutting's "Furniture Treasury." Antique white and gold decoration or mahogany.

Overall size 23 x 30. Plate 20 x 24.

No. M839 Chair

Reproduced from an original Sheraton chair now in the Baker collection. Natural beech, antique white or antique black and gold.

Width 21. Depth 19. Height 33.

No. M839 Dressing Table

Adapted from a Chinese side table illustrated in "Chinese Furniture" published in London by Benn Brothers, Ltd. Leather top. Antique white and gold decoration or mahogany.

Top 19 x 42. Height 30.

No. M740 Powder Table

Adapted from a late 18th Century Sheraton console formerly in the possession of an antique dealer in Brompton Road, London, England. Boxwood inlays.

Width 36. Depth 18½. Height 28½.

No. M839½ Chest

Adapted from a Hepplewhite chest-on-chest at Denston Hall, England.

Top 18 x 36. Height 55.

No. M729 Wall Mirror

Reproduced from one purchased in France,
and now in the Baker collection. Mahogany
and Gold.

Overall Size 26 x 40.   Plate 20 x 26.

No. M729 Chair

English Regency. Adapted from an original
pair purchased from an antique dealer in
Brompton Road, London, England. These
chairs are now in the Baker collection.
Black and Gold.

Width 18.   Depth 19.   Height 32.

No. M729 Dresser Base

Adapted from a Mahogany bureau of Sheraton style illustrated in "American Antique
Furniture" by Edgar G. Miller, Jr. Circa
1795-1810. Boxwood inlays.

Top 21 x 42.   Height 35.

No. M729 Night Table

Reproduced from an early 19th Century
sewing table recently sold by the American
Art Galleries, New York City. Boxwood inlays.

Top closed 16 x 16.   Open 16 x 31.
Height 28.

No. M729 Bed

The motifs of this bed were reproduced
from an early 19th Century chair purchased
from a New York importer of antiques and
now in the Baker collection. Mahogany or
Black and Gold.

Twin or Full size.   Headboard Height 42.
Footboard Height 26.

No. M729 Dressing Table Mirror

Reproduced from an antique mirror of the Hepplewhite school bought from John A. Pearson, an antique dealer in South Kensington, London, England. The original is now in the Baker collection. Antique Gold or Antique Pine.

Overall Size 20 x 42. Plate 18 x 26.

No. M730 Mirror

Reproduced from an imported yew-wood and gold mirror purchased in England and now in the Baker collection. Mahogany and Gold or Yew-wood and Gold.

Overall Size 2¹ x 37. Plate 16 x 24.

NOTE: No. M740 Mirror same design. Plate 20 x 30.

No. M729 Dressing Table

Adapted from a writing desk designed by Sheraton for Carlton House, London, England. Circa 1790, Boxwood inlays. Available with or without metal gallery.

Top 20 x 42. Height 30.

Note: No. M729½ Dressing Table same piece with leather top.

No. M729 Bench

Adapted from an early 19th Century footstool illustrated in "Regency Furniture" by M. Jourdain, and from the collection of Edward Hudson, Esq. Black and Gold.

Width 14. Length 31. Height 22. Seat Height 17.

No. M729½ Chest

Adapted from a Hepplewhite tall chest illustrated in his book "Cabinet Maker's and Upholsterer's Guide," published in 1794.

Top 19 x 37. Height 50.

No. M739 Wall Mirror

Reproduced from a carved rope mirror in a private collection at Aberystwyth, Wales. Antique Gold.

Overall Size 28 x 39.   Plate 26 x 30.

No. M739 Night Table

Adapted from a Sheraton style washstand in the Metropolitan Museum of Art. Circa 1800-1820.

Top 14 x 18.   Height including gallery 32. Gallery 5 in.

No. M739 Dresser Base

Reproduced from a swell front chest of drawers of the Hepplewhite school illustrated in Edgar G. Miller, Jr.'s "American Antique Furniture". Circa 1785-1800. Boxwood inlays.

Top 21 x 42.   Height including gallery 37.   Gallery 2 in.

No. M739 Bench

Motifs taken from an Empire X bench at Syon House, England. Circa 1785. Mahogany.

Top 21 x 16.   Height 19.

No. M739 Bed

Adapted from a Mahogany sleigh bed illustrated in "Colonial Furniture in America" by Luke Vincent Lockwood. Boxwood inlays.

Twin or Full size.   Headboard height 37 Footboard height 27.

No. M730 Bench

Reproduced from a simplified American settee from the collection of Mr. Wm. M. Ellicott and illustrated in "American Antique Furniture" by Edgar G. Miller, Jr. Circa 1810-1820. Black and Gold.

Width 16. Length 41. Height 20.
Seat Height 16.

No. M739 Dressing Table

Adapted from a Sheraton writing table in the possession of an English antique dealer and illustrated in the Connoisseur Magazine. The mirror was reproduced from one on a Mahogany chest of drawers owned by The Albany Institute and Historical and Art Society. Boxwood inlays.

Top 20 x 39. Height Overall 50.
Table Height 29. Plate 16 x 22.

NOTE: No. M739½ Dressing Table same piece without mirror and with leather top.

No. M739 Chair

Reproduced from a late Sheraton chair purchased in England and now in the Baker collection. Circa 1810. Mahogany or painted and decorated.

Width 19. Depth 20. Height 32.

No. M740½ Chest

Adapted from an original Hepplewhite chest of drawers purchased in London, England, and now in the Baker collection. Boxwood inlays.

Top 20 x 34. Height including mirrored gallery 61.
Plate 8 x 32.

NOTE: No. M739½ Chest same piece without mirrored gallery. Height 51.

No. M429 Wall Mirror

Adapted from an English Hepplewhite mirror illustrated in Wallace Nutting's book, "Furniture Treasury," and now in the possession of F. Sanderson. Antique gold.
Plate 20 x 30.   Height 43.

No. M439 Bench

Adapted from a stool illustrated by George Hepplewhite in his book, "Cabinetmakers' and Upholsterers' Guide," published in 1794.
Top 19 x 19.   Height 17.

No. M447 Dresser Base

Adapted from a chest of drawers at Bayfordbury, Herts, England. Yew-wood banding.
Top 22 x 44.   Height 34.

No. M445 Night Table

Adapted from an original stand in the collection of E. Marshall-Hale, Esq.
Top 13 x 16.   Height 26.

No. M448 Canopy Bed

Adapted from a Hepplewhite "Field" bed in an English collection. Twin or full size. Black and Gold or Mahogany.
Overall Height 76.

No. M439 Chair
Adapted from a late 18th Century chair, illustrated in the "Dictionary of English Furniture" by Percy MacQuoid.
Width 18½. Depth 18½. Height 25½.

No. M446 Bed
Adapted from the motifs in a Sheraton "Drawing Room Chair" of the early 19th Century. Black and Gold or Mahogany. Twin or full size.
Headboard 39. Footboard 25.

No. M445 Dressing Table Mirror
Adapted from a Hepplewhite mirror illustrated by T. A. Strange in his book, "English Furniture." Antique Gold.
Plate 17 x 23½. Overall 39 x 22.

No. M447½ Chest
Adapted from a Hepplewhite tall chest illustrated in his book "Cabinet Maker's and Upholsterer's Guide," published in 1794.
Top 19 x 37. Height 50.

No. M445 Dressing Table
Adapted from a small bow-front side table of Hepplewhite design. Circa 1785. Yew-wood banding.
Top 20½ x 44. Height 30.

No. M809 Sideboard

Reproduced from a Hepplewhite sideboard illustrated in T. A. Strange's "English Furniture during the 18th Century." A similar model is now in a private Eastern collection.

Width 72. Depth 26. Height 36.

No. M809 Arm Chair

Reproduced from a mahogany chair — the property of Mr. Humphrey Lee.

Width 24. Depth 23. Height 38.

No. M809 Server

Adapted from an 18th Century dressing table in the property of George Dando, England.

Top 19 x 36. Height, including Gallery, 35.

No. M809 Chair

Reproduced from a mahogany chair — the
property of Mr. Humphrey Lee.
Width 19.   Depth 21.   Height 37.

No. M809 Cabinet

Adopted from a Hepplewhite breakfront
bookcase imported from England and
recently sold at a New York antique sale.
Width 48.   Depth 14.   Height 76.

No. M809 Table

The details of this table were reproduced
from an original antique model in the possession of Mr. John Milton Quaintance.
Top 44 x 66.   Height 29.   8-foot extension.

No. M819 Sideboard

Adapted from the base of a Georgian
breakfront bookcase in the collection of
Mrs. H. Hope of London, England. Circa
1795.

Width 64.   Depth 19.   Height 37.

No. M819 Arm Chair

Reproduced from a Lyre-back chair illustrated in "Furniture Masterpieces of Duncan
Phyfe" by Charles Over Cornelius.

Width 22.   Depth 23.   Height 35.

No. M819 Server

Reproduced from an 18th Century server in
the collection of a Brompton Road antique
dealer, London, England.

Top 19 x 38.   Height 32.

No. M819 Chair
Reproduced from a Lyre-back chair illustrated in "Furniture Masterpieces of Duncan Phyfe" by Charles Over Cornelius.
Width 19. Depth 21. Height 34.

No. M819 Cabinet
Sheraton, about 1800, from the collection of Mrs. Percy MacQuoid, London, England.
Width 40. Depth 14. Height 75.

No. M819 Table
The pedestal of this table was reproduced from a Sheraton drum table of the late 18th Century.
Top 50 x 71. Height 29. 8 ft. Extension.
NOTE: No. M819½ Table same Table with rectangular top 50 x 71.

No. M709 Sideboard

A reproduction of a Hepplewhite sideboard
in a private English collection. Boxwood
inlays.

Top 24 x 69.   Height 36.

No. M709 Arm Chair

Reproduced from an original Mahogany
chair with carved ornament in the collection
of Colonel Osborn, The Red House, Surrey,
England. Circa 1795-1800. Mahogany or
Black and Gold.

Width 22.   Depth 23.   Height 35.

No. M709 Server

Reproduced from a 19th Century card table
in the collection of L. J. Schermerhorn, a
similar model of which is illustrated in
"American Antique Furniture" by Edgar G
Miller, Jr. Circa 1830-1840.

Top closed 18 x 36.   Open 36 x 36.
Height 28.

No. M709 Chair

Reproduced from an original Mahogany
chair with carved ornament in the collection
of Colonel Osborn, The Red House, Surrey,
England. Circa 1795-1800. Mahogany or
Black and Gold.

Width 19. Depth 20. Height 33.

No. M709 Cabinet

The details of this cabinet were copied from
a Hepplewhite escritoire bookcase illustrated in MacQuoid's "The Age of Satinwood"
and the property of Robert Eastwood, Esq.
England. Circa 1773. Boxwood inlays.

Base 16 x 40. Height 72.

No. M709 Table

A dining table typical of the type made by
Thomas Sheraton in England and in America
by Duncan Phyfe during the early part of
the 19th Century. Boxwood inlay.

Top 44 x 66. Height 29½.
8-ft. Extension.

No. M719½ Sideboard

Reproduced from an original sideboard illustrated in Wallace Nutting's "Furniture Treasury" from the collection of I. Sack. Circa 1790. Boxwood inlays.

Top 25 x 72.   Height including deck 41½.

NOTE: No. M719 Sideboard same piece without gallery deck. Height 37.

No. M719 Arm Chair

Reproduced from an early 19th Century chair purchased from a New York importer of antiques and now in the Baker collection. Mahogany or Black and Gold.

Width 22.   Depth 22.   Height 34.

No. M719 Server

Adapted from a tray top table purchased from an Eastern collector and now a part of the Baker collection. Boxwood inlay.

Top 19 x 36.   Height including gallery 32.
Gallery 3 in.

No. M719 Chair

Reproduced from an early 19th Century
chair purchased from a New York importer
of antiques and now in the Baker collection.
Mahogany or Black and Gold.

Width 19. Depth 21. Height 33.

No. M719 Cabinet

Adapted from a Sheraton bookcase at "The
Treasure House," Preston, England. Boxwood
inlays.

Base 16 x 48. Height 80.

No. M719 Table

Reproduced from an early 19th Century
table illustrated in the Connoisseur Magazine. Boxwood inlay.

Top 44 x 66. Height 29½. 8-ft. extension.

No. M720 Sideboard

Adapted from the base of a late 18th Century breakfront bookcase recently sold at a New York antique sale. Boxwood inlays.

Top 19 x 63.   Height including gallery 37½
Gallery 2½ in.

No. M409 Chair

Reproduced from an antique model found in the old "Fairbanks House," Dedham, Mass. Similar model illustrated in Strange's "English Furniture during the 18th Century."

Width 20½.   Depth 20.   Height 36.

No. M409 Arm Chair

Reproduced from an antique model found in the old "Fairbanks House," Dedham, Mass. Similar model illustrated in Strange's "English Furniture during the 18th Century."

Width 24.   Depth 22.   Height 37.

No. M720 Chest Server

Reproduced from a Hepplewhite chest of drawers in the collection of a Chicago antique dealer. Boxwood inlays. Pull-out slide under top.

Top 20 x 35.   Height 35

No. M720 Arm Chair
Reproduced from a shield back Hepple-
white chair illustrated in Edgar G. Miller,
Jr.'s "American Antique Furniture." Circa
1780-1790.
Width 25. Depth 22. Height 38.

No. M720 Chair
Reproduced from a shield back Hepple
white chair illustrated in Edgar G. Miller,
Jr.'s "American Antique Furniture." Circa
1780-1790.
Width 19. Depth 20. Height 38.

No. M720 Corner Cabinet
The details of this cabinet were copied from
an American corner cabinet illustrated in
Wallace Nutting's "Furniture Treasury."
Circa 1780-1800. Boxwood inlays.
Base 19 x 38. Height 77.

No. M419 Table
Adapted from a Sheraton three-part table
illustrated by L. V. Lockwood in "Colonial
Furniture in America." Yew-wood banding.
Table closed 70 x 44. Open 106 x 44.
Height 29½.
Center section open 62 x 44. Closed 26 x 44.
Console ends — Width 44. Depth 22.
NOTE: Table closes as No. 1689 — see
Page 86.

No. M424 Sideboard
Adapted from a Georgian piece in the collection of Mrs. H. Hope of London, England Circa 1795. Yew-wood banding.
Top 19 x 66. Height 36.

No. M410 Chair
Adapted from a Hepplewhite chair purchased in England from an antique dealer in Queens Road, Dalston, London, England and now in the Baker collection.
Width 19½. Depth 20. Height 37.

No. M410 Arm Chair
Adapted from a Hepplewhite chair purchased in England from an antique dealer in Queens Road, Dalston, London, England, and now in the Baker collection.
Width 24. Depth 22. Height 38.

No. M424 Server
Reproduced from an original antique folding top table purchased in England and now a part of the Baker collection. Circa 1795. Yew-wood bandings.
Top closed 17 x 36. Top open 34 x 36.
Height 29.

No. M422 Mirror

Reproduced from a Georgian mirror in a private Eastern collection. Antique Pine. Antique Gold or Gold Leaf.

Overall 34 x 54.

No. M424 Cabinet

An adaptation of a late 18th Century bookcase, detailed from T. A. Strange's "Furniture, Woodwork and Decoration of the 18th Century."

Base 14 x 49. Height 72½.

No. M425 Table

Copied from an English 18th Century table owned by a New York importer. Circa 1779. Yew-wood inlay.

Top 44 x 66. Height 29½.
8-foot Extension.

NOTE: No. M425½ Table same piece without yew-wood inlay.

No. M107 Sideboard

Reproduced from a sideboard illustrated in
Thos. Sheraton's book, "The Cabinet Maker
and Upholsterer's Drawing Book."
Top 25 x 72.   Height 36.

No. M421 Side Chair

Reproduced from a three ladder back chair
illustrated in Wallace Nutting's "Furniture
Treasury."
Width 21.   Depth 22.   Height 37.

No. M421 Arm Chair

Reproduced from a three ladder back chair
illustrated in Wallace Nutting's "Furniture
Treasury."
Width 23.   Depth 23.   Height 38.

No. M107 Table

Reproduced from an English 18th Century
antique table in the possession of a New
York importer. Circa 1780.
Top 44 x 66.   8-foot Extension.

No. M89 Arm Chair
Reproduced from an antique in a private English collection, which was sold by the American Art Association at an antique auction.

Width 24. Depth 23. Height 37.

NOTE: No. M89½ Arm Chair same chair upholstered over the rail.

No. M89 Chair
Reproduced from an antique in a private English collection, which was sold by the American Art Association at an antique auction.

Width 21. Depth 21. Height 36.

NOTE: No. M89½ Chair same chair upholstered over the rail.

No. M107 Cabinet
Adapted from a cabinet illustrated in the Connoisseur Magazine and in the possession of John Bell of Aberdeen, Scotland.

Base 19 x 34. Height 77.

No. M413 Table
Adapted from an original of Sheraton design illustrated in "Arts and Decorations."

Top 44 x 66. Height 29.
8-foot Extension.

No. M820 Chair

Reproduced from a Duncan Phyfe chair in the Metropolitan Museum, New York.
Width 20. Depth 21. Height 34.

No. M820 Sideboard

Adapted from an "Oxford" sideboard in a private Eastern collection.
Width 57. Depth 19. Height 34.

No. M820 Arm Chair

Reproduced from a Duncan Phyfe chair in the Metropolitan Museum, New York.
Width 23. Depth 23. Height 36.

No. M820 Table

Adapted from a Sheraton drum table of the late 18th Century.
Top 46 x 54. Height 29. 8 ft. Extension.
NOTE: Table equipped with hinged drop legs for support when extended.

No. M820 Corner Cabinet

Adapted from an 18th Century English corner cupboard imported from England and now in a private Eastern collection.
Mahogany or Pine.
Base 16 x 30. Height 74.

This choice mahogany sideboard, *The Severton*, is indicative of the rare pieces to be found in the Manor House collection. The original was in the collection of Sir John Hall and was made about 1812.

The MANOR HOUSE
383 Madison Avenue
NEW YORK CITY

A Special Division of Baker Furniture, Inc. Devoted to the Manufacture of the Finest Hand Made and Custom Finished Reproductions

The following pages show a few selections which are typical of the complete Manor House Collection.

ONCE in a while the collector of antiques will find a piece that warrants a special place in his collection. Fine though his other pieces are, this one will be still better — its depth and richness of color will be greater; it will have more finely executed detail and carving; its general character will stamp it as an extraordinary piece. The reproductions in the Manor House collection bear a similar relationship to those in the regular Baker line. They are "gem" pieces. In making them there is no restriction in the effort to produce the finest reproductions possible.

Upper Left: **The Berkeley Chair** is typical of the many distinquished chairs in the **Manor House** collection. Every detail of its unusual contours, exceptionally fine carving and color was duplicated from the rare original found in High Wycombe, near London, England.

Lower Left. A living room completely furnished with **Manor House Reproductions.**

Above: **The Crichton Breakfront Secretary-Bookcase.** No piece typifies the dignity and charm of the Georgian era quite so much as a "breakfront." This is a particularly fine copy of a late model. The doors are fitted with crown glass, used in all Manor House pieces where glass is required, (described on page 8) and the writing bed is lined with fine tooled leather.

Prices and further information regarding **Manor** *House furniture will be sent upon request*

THE MANOR HOUSE
383 Madison Avenue
New York
TRUE REPLICAS

Right: Manor House reproductions in a pine-panelled living room. The important Chippendale chest to the left has a graceful serpentine front. The corner posts are ornamented with finely carved details. The mirror above this chest, Chippendale in style, clearly indicates the work of a master carver. It is finished in antique gold leaf. The Chippendale sofa is from an English antique, which has been modified for comfort. To the left of the sofa is an extraordinarily fine 18th Century rope-carved chair.

The Randolph Secretary-Bookcase. A fine secretary-bookcase which is a copy of an English original that was brought to this country about twenty-five years ago by a New York dealer. Like all Manor House reproductions, the doors are fitted with crown glass. The writing bed is lined with fine leather, bordered with a traditional motif, tooled in gold leaf.

Few pieces of furniture add more sparkle to a room than a rare Georgian gold-leaf mirror. In the Manor House collection are several of similar character to that illustrated above, which is carved by hand and finished with genuine gold leaf. The *Noble Commode*, below it, was copied from an original in the collection of Frank Noble, Esq. It is of the Sheraton school.

Prices and further information regarding Manor House furniture will be sent upon request

English Dining Room furniture of outstanding character is a special feature of the Manor House collection. *The Albert Table*, shown above, is an early nineteenth century piece of unusual proportions and detail. The original is owned by John Gross, Esq., of Bethlehem, Pennsylvania, an American collector.

ALTHOUGH one essential for Manor House furniture lies in the selection of designs requiring intricate craftsmanship, there are other important indications of the high standards set for this furniture. Not only is the furniture itself made by hand, but the brasses are also, and wherever glass is used, that, too, is made by hand. The finish of each piece is done individually by an artist and every care and effort is made to follow the work of the past as closely as possible.

Left: The Birmingham Commode. The original was a rare piece, as is this reproduction. Chippendale of the Mid-Georgian period. *Above: The Willoughby.* Unique Regency Secretary-Bookcase with bowed and recessed center. Made in mahogany or satinwood. Crown glass in doors and writing bed lined with polished leather, tooled in gold leaf. There is a brass dividing strip between the two center doors as in the original.

Prices and further information regarding Manor House furniture will be sent upon request

Top right: The Taylor Console and Coleshill Mirror. A late 18th Century console or carving board in mahogany with inlaid lines of yew wood; surmounted by a rococo mirror of Chippendale character in gold leaf. Hand made copies of English originals.
Top, left: The Watkins Chest. "French" Hepplewhite at its best, this Manor House replica has unusually pleasing form and restraint in ornamentation. By courtesy of Norman Powell Pendley, Esq., of Atlanta, Ga. The chairs are from the Baker collection of Regency furniture. Right, center: The Oxford Chair, a graceful chair, also of "French" Hepplewhite origin, that is a gem of form and proportion. Shown with the Barham Mahogany Commode, from the Manor House Collection.
Above: The Seymour Commode, is described by the dealer in Sevenoaks, England, from whom the original was obtained, as "a fine Hepplewhite bow front mahogany small cupboard with two doors, circa 1785. Purchased from R. Glover, Esq., The Old Town House, Haslemere, Surrey." Bottom, right: The Edwards Whatnot and Shelburne Chair. The whatnot is of early 19th Century lineage, finished in black or antique green paint with gold lines. The chair is one of the best examples of Sheraton style. Each is copied from an original found in England.

Prices and further information regarding Manor House furniture will be sent upon request

The Chelsea Overmantel Mirror

Seldom does one find a reproduction of the unusual type of this hand carved Chippendale overmantel mirror. With its somewhat elaborate ornamentation and brackets for choice objets d'art, it is intended to serve as a focal point in a more formal type of Georgian room. The Chelsea is available in antique pine or gold leaf finish.

The Geffrye Sideboard

From the Geffrye Museum, Shoreditch, England this dignified yet simple sideboard takes its name. The piece has a peculiar charm, devoid as it is, of all ornamentation. For its beauty, it relies upon its superb line and proportion, its excellent depth of color and finish and the ten fine brass oval pulls.

Prices and further information regarding **Manor House** *furniture will be sent upon request*

Specifications for a Masterpiece

As it is impossible to evaluate the worth of a fine painting in terms of material specifications, so does the beauty and value of choice reproductions elude reduction to such terms. Even the camera is only partially able to reproduce the many nuances of design and finish which contribute to the intangible beauty of a masterpiece of furniture craftsmanship. Thus, the illustrations on these pages are intended merely to indicate the general character and extent of the designs in the Manor House collection.

Top: The Wedgewood Commode, **reproduced from a New York collection, made in paint (as original), or rosewood (as shown); with marble or wood top.** *Center: Preston Table with Holborn Chairs.* **The former a copy of a distinguished Chippendale game table and the chairs reproduced from a unique model in the South Kensington Museum, made—or inspired — by Robert Manwaring.**
Bottom, left: The Thackerey Gallery Table. **An exquisite model in Chippendale style, taken from an English original. Treatment of gallery and carved detail is exceptionally fine.** *Lower Right: The Brighton Desk.* **The Brighton kidney shaped desk is one of the more versatile of our 18th Century designs, and can be used with any style from Queen Anne to Regency. Made in walnut or mahogany with genuine gold-leaf tooling on leather top. Reproduced from one of the rarest pieces of its type.**

Prices and further information regarding Manor House furniture will be sent upon request

A Division of Baker Furniture, Inc.

The Manor House Collection

is recognized as America's best group of reproductions.

As has been said before, each piece of Manor House furniture is made and finished by hand. Crown glass (also hand made) is used in the glass doors of all cabinets and all hardware is specially made and hand-burnished. The designs are chosen for their unusual character and fineness of carving and other detail. Manor House furniture is craftsmanship—unexcelled.

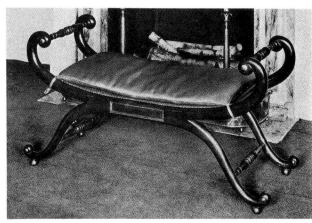

Top: The Crawford Drum Table. A unique, large Sheraton drum table, 50″ in diameter. Copied from an English original formerly in the Baker Collection. *Top left: The Melson Chair.* A scroll-back Chippendale chair with paw feet. Original from Shoreditch, London, England. *Above: The Rawson Bench.* Copied from an original found in England and brought to this country. Regency. *Left: The Kean Cabinet.* Late 18th Century. Characteristic of Sheraton in lightness of scale and fineness of inlay. *Right: The Chelton Whatnot.* Rare in an original and rarer still as a reproduction. Elaborately Georgian. The original was an English piece from a collection in Atlanta, Georgia.

Prices and further information regarding Manor House furniture will be sent upon request

Index to Pattern Numbers—Connoisseur Furniture

For quick reference, all patterns are listed below in
numerical order with corresponding catalog pages.

Index to Pattern Numbers—Milling Road Shop

For quick reference, all patterns are listed below in
numerical order with corresponding catalog pages.

Price Guide

This price guide represents an educated estimate of the prices a consumer could expect to pay for the items represented in this book. It assumes that they are found in excellent condition and without blemish, refinishing, or repair. The prices can vary greatly depending on condition, the region of the country in which they are bought, and the type of outlet. The buyer should always carefully examine a piece before purchase, and if in doubt, pass it by. The best resource is a trustworthy and reputable dealer.

The values are organized by page number (the left column) and by position on the page (the middle column). They represent prices as of Fall, 1996.

Page	Pos	Price
6	R	2200
10	TL	2200
	BL	475
	TR	575
	CR	400 ea.
	BR	500
11	TR	750
	C	250
	BL	450
	TR	900
	BL	400
12	TL	450
	TC	150
	BL	1800
	TR	200
	BR	425
13	TL	400
	C	650
	BL	650
	TR	425
	BR	500
14	TL	1200
	C	350
	BL	400
	TR	300
	BR	450
15	TL	650
	C	350
	BL	350
	TR	350
	BR	600
16	TL	1000
	CL	250
	BL	400
	TR	350
	BR	1900
17	TL	1400
	C	375
	BL	375
	TR	450
	BR	550
18	TL	700
	C	250
	BL	600
	TR	350
	BR	600
19	TL	550
	CL	400
	BL	350

Page	Pos	Price
	TR	200
	BR	1800
20	TL	900
	C	300
	BL	300
	TR	450
	BR	550
21	TL	1000
	CL	2500
	BL	400
	TR	350
	BC	100
	BR	900
22	TL	3500
	BL	350
	TR	400
	CR	300
	BR	500
23	TL	700
	C	200
	BL	1000
	TR	350
	BR	1800
24	TL	950
	C	400
	BL	375
	TR	400
	BR	1400
25	TL	700
	CL	350
	BL	400
	TR	450
	BR	1600
26	TL	450
	BL	1800
	TR	300
	CR	350
	BR	350
27	TL	950
	C	350
	BL	300
	TR	400
	BR	1400
28	TL	650
	CL	350
	BL	650
	TR	600
	CR	500
	BR	350

Page	Pos	Price
29	TL	300
	CL	250
	BL	350
	TR	700
	CR	250
	BR	275
30	TL	400
	CL	300
	BL	350
	TR	340
	CR	250
	BR	450
31	BL	600
	CL	300
	BL	275
	TR	450
	CR	300
	BR	500
32	TL	950
	C	200
	BL	300
	TR	600
	BR	250
33	TL	1200
	C	200
	BL	500
	TR	250
	BR	400
34	TC	950
	BL	1800
	CR	250
	BR	250
35	TL	950
	C	400
	BL	600
	TR	900
	CR	200
	BR	700
36	TL	1200
	CL	250
	BL	350
	TR	300
	CR	250
	BR	900
37	TL	450
	CR	400
	BL	550
	TR	600
	CR	300
38	TL	400
	C	250
	BL	500
	TR	950
	BR	300
39	TL	900
	C	250
	BL	300
	TR	400
	BR	350
40	TL	550
	C	350
	BR	1000
41	TL	350
	CL	500
	BL	300
	TR	650
	CR	400
	BR	1200
42	BL	350
	C	450
	BL	1200
	TR	350

Page	Pos	Price
	CR	500
	BR	350
43	TL	2200
	BL	350
	TR	275
	CR	250
	BR	900
44	TL	600
	CL	500
	BL	350
	TR	250
	BR	1800
45	TL	450
	C	250
	BL	350
	TR	450
	BC	300
	BR	900
46	TL	700
	CL	350
	BL	650
	TR	1700
	BR	350
47	TL	550
	CL	300
	BL	1200
	TR	575
	CR	300
	BR	900
48	TL	1200
	C	350
	BL	1200
	TR	550
	BR	375
49	TL	450
	CL	350
	BL	750
	TR	250
	BR	750
50	TL	650
	C	450
	BL	1200
	TR	1800
	BR	550
51	TL	1800
	CL	350
	BL	750
	TR	450
	BR	400
52	TL	950
	C	250
	BL	350
	TR	300
	BR	650
53	TL	1600
	BL	350
	TR	400
	CR	600
	BR	800
54	TL	750
	C	550
	BL	600
	TR	1200
	BR	600
55	TL	450
	C	300
	BL	600
	TC	750
	TR	950
	BR	350
56	TL	750
	C	350

Page	Pos	Price
	BL	350
	TR	300
	BC	275
	BR	400
57	TL	350
	CL	250
	BL	300
	TR	450
	CR	250
	BR	600
58	TL	400
	C	250
	BL	600
	TC	300
	TR	375
	BR	600
59	TL	350
	C	300
	BL	450
	TC	375
	TR	250
	BR	800
60	TL	1800
	BL	250
	TC	250
	TR	300
	CR	300
	BR	650
62	TC	1600
	BL	450
	BR	750
63	TL	400
	BC	700
	TL	1500
64	TL	1800
	BL	475
	TR	400
	BR	1200
65	TL	500
	CL	400
	BC	1200
	TR	1800
66	TL	1800
	BL	375
	TR	300
	BR	675
67	TL	600
	CL	450
	BL	1400
	TR	1600
68	TL	1400
	BL	550
	TR	350
	BR	500
69	TL	600
	CL	400
	BL	1200
	TR	1600
70	TC	1500
	C	600
	BL	700
	BR	400
71	TL	350
	CL	550
	BC	1000
	TR	1500
72	TL	1400
	BL	750
	TR	550
	BR	675
73	TL	500
	CL	400

Page	Pos	Price
	BC	1200
	TR	1800
74	TL	1400
	BL	600
	TR	400
	BR	1000
75	TL	550
	BL	1000
	CR	1200
76	TL	1400
	BL	600
	TR	400
	BR	600
77	TL	500
	CL	300
	BC	1200
	TR	1200
78	TC	850
	C	450
	BL	600
	BR	300
79	TL	450
	CL	300
	BC	1000
	TR	1000
80	TL	1500
	BL	500
	TR	400
	BR	700
81	TL	450
	CL	300
	BC	1000
	TR	1500
82	TL	1300
	BL	450
	TR	300
	BR	600
83	TL	450
	CL	300
	BC	950
	TR	950
84	TL	750
	CL	300
	TR	450
	CR	900
85	TL	450
	CL	300
	BC	950
	TR	950
86	TL	800
	BL	500
	CR	350
	BR	1200
87	TL	450
	C	300
	TR	1700
	BC	1200
88	TL	750
	BL	350
	TR	500
	BR	950
89	TL	500
	CL	350
	BL	900
	TR	1600
90	TL	1200
	CL	550
	TR	300
	BR	900
91	TL	500
	C	550
	BL	1400

	TR	1400		BL	250		CL	450	138	TL	250		BC	200	168	TC	1800
	BR	450		TR	300		TR	300		CL	350		BR	350		BL	650
92	TL	1200		BR	575		BR	600		BL	350	151	TL	400		CR	575
	CL	500	107	TL	100	121	TL	350		TR	300		C	350	169	TL	275
	BL	500		CL	500		BL	900		BR	1800		BL	650		BC	1400
	TR	300		BL	1400		TR	900	139	Tl	1000		TR	400		TR	1400
	BR	1800		TR	200		BR	200		CL	250		BR	775	170	TL	750
93	TL	1400		BR	1200	122	TL	600		BL	550	152	TL	700		BL	550
	CL	600	108	TL	350		BL	400		TR	500		BL	200		TR	350
	BL	700		CL	100		TR	250		CR	300		TR	250		BR	675
	TR	425		BC	450		BR	200	140	TL	500		BR	500	171	TL	475
	BR	1500		TR	350	123	TL	350		CL	350	153	TL	200		C	275
94	TL	900		CR	250		CL	200		BL	600		CL	775		BC	1400
	C	550	110	TL	600		BL	700		TR	300		BL	175		TR	2000
	BL	450		C	150		TR	750		BC	300		TR	175	172	TL	750
	TR	350		BL	350	124	TL	800		BR	2000		BR	600		BL	475
	BR	650		TR	350		BL	350	141	TL	400	154	TL	250		TR	300
95	TL	1000		BC	100		TR	500		CL	300		CL	400		BR	600
	C	650		BR	300		BR	300		BL	500		BL	200	173	TL	250
	BL	300	111	TL	600	125	TL	400		TC	300		TR	350		BC	1400
	TR	450		C	200		CL	250		TR	400		BR	450		TR	1400
	BR	900		BL	300		BC	500		BR	900	155	TL	150	174	TL	1600
96	TL	1800		TR	250		TR	550	142	TL	650		CL	350		CL	450
	BL	600		BR	150	126	TL	500		C	175		BL	350		TR	275
	TR	700	112	TL	250		BL	400		BL	200		TR	275		BR	1400
	CR	450		C	150		TR	250		TC	150		BR	700	175	Tl	500
	BR	950		BL	400		BR	300		TR	100	156	TL	225		C	300
98	TL	350		TC	200	127	CL	300		BR	350		CL	600		BC	1200
	CL	1000		TR	350		BC	350	143	TL	300		BL	450		TR	1200
	BL	350		BR	300		TR	400		C	300		TR	125	176	TL	750
	TR	200	113	TL	550	128	TL	150		BL	150		BR	450		C	650
	CR	250		C	200		CL	600		TR	400	157	TL	350		BL	900
	BR	775		BL	300		BL	250		BC	150		CL	675		TR	350
99	TL	200		TR	500		TR	110		BR	500		BL	200		BR	1600
	BL	2000		CR	150		CR	100	144	TL	1200		TR	400	177	TC	900
	TR	300		BR	550		BR	300		C	300		BR	750	178	TL	750
	CR	600	114	TL	500	129	TL	500		BL	250	158	TL	250		BL	500
	BR	500		BL	450		C	250		TR	400		CL	500		BR	3500
100	TL	300		TC	250		BL	200		BC	200		BL	150	179	CL	2200
	CL	900		TR	300		TR	900		BR	550		TR	350		CR	400
	BL	250		BC	200		BR	300	145	TL	350		BR	500		BR	900
	TR	700		BR	450	130	TL	200		C	250	159	TL	900	180	TL	1800
	CR	150	115	TL	400		BL	300		BL	350		BL	200		CL	300
	BR	600		C	200		TR	250		TR	200		TR	300		BL	500
101	TL	200		BL	300		C	200		BR	750		BR	950		BR	1800
	CL	450		TR	350		CR	200	146	TL	500	160	TL	150	181	TL	
	BL	1500		BR	750		BR	400		C	300		CL	500		(mirror)	450
	TC	250	116	TL	600	131	TL	200		BL	300		BL	275		TL	
	TR	1800		C	400		CL	450		TR	250		TR	175		(chest)	900
	BR	500		BL	350		BL	200		BC	150		BR	600		CL	600
102	TL	200		TR	400		TR	650		BR	200	161	TL	165		TR	
	TC	1000		BC	350		C	175	147	TL	450		BL	800		(console)	500
	BL	250		BR	300		BR	350		CL	200		TR	500		CR	425
	TR	400	117	TL	400	132	TL	250		BL	200		BR	500		RB	300,400
	CR	200		CR	400		CL	600		TC	250	162	TC	1400	182	TC	450
	BR	550		BL	250		BL	150		TR	200		BL	1000		BR	1400
103	TL	200		TR	400		TR	250		CR	250		BR	500	183	LB	500
	BL	2200		CR	200		BR	300		BR	550	163	TL	350		TR	450
	TR	450		BR	300	133	TL	200	148	RL	350		BC	1000		CL	300,500,
	BR	550	118	TL	450		BL	650		CL	300		TR	1600			500
104	TL	350		BL	550		TR	200		BL	450	164	TC	750		BR	500,500
	CL	1000		TC	350		CR	500		TR	450		BL	375	184	TL	375
	BL	500		TR	350		BR	350		BR	1650		BR	575		BL	450
	TR	300		BC	200	134	TL	400	149	TL	500	165	TL	250		TR	675
	CR	250		BR	450		CL	600		C	300		BC	900		CR	350
	BR	375	119	TL	450		BL	125		BL	850		TR	1400		BC	500
105	TL	350		CL	250		TR	200		TR	250	166	TC	1600			
	BL	1200		BL	350		BR	350		BR	300		BL	350			
	TR	250		TR	650	135	TL	250	150	TL	650		BR	475			
	BR	1200		BC	350		BL	600		C	600	167	TL	275			
106	TL	200		BR	200		TR	300		BL	325		BC	1400			
	CL	1000	120	TL	800		BR	375		TR	300		TR	1400			